I0458833

God, Mommy and Me
Our Unscripted Conversations

A 42-Week Journey for Expectant Mothers

Dr. KB

DEDICATION

To every woman who wondered, *"what if I had only embraced this sacred journey,"* to you this book is a song of Zion—**a song of redemption**. An unborn child bears a record of heaven's approval and an expectant mother's womb houses a living soul that transports God's breath and His image. This transaction is sacred! The approval to exit the stage midway or at the beginning of the journey disrupts a holy scene. As your unborn child's breath was prematurely hushed, angelic beings were dismissed, and their assignments were cancelled. Nonetheless, the ultimate sacrifice of love included you and me, and there is nothing that we can do to stop our Heavenly Father from loving His children—*and that is the power of redemption!*

TO MY READERS

This manuscript was written under divine inspiration, so the conversations remain untouched to honor the integrity of the inspired language. It is a three-part conversation which includes the voices of the unborn, the expectant mother, and the divine instructions rooted in God's word. The conversations are sobering and underscores the direct connection between the sacredness of an unborn child's life and eternal life. The divine instructions toggle between instructions that are for the expectant mother and at times given to both mom and her unborn. Most of the instructions are direct messages to remind the expectant mother that she has been chosen to mold the outcome of a human's life.

The conversations are written in the following order:

Dear Mom: The Voice of the Unborn speaking to the expectant mother.

Dear Child: The Voice of Mom speaking to her unborn child.

Dear Children: The Voice of God inspired wisdom speaking to the unborn child and/or expectant mother.

The Unborn's voice is supported by medical research and is recorded to amplify the sacredness of life at each stage of a pregnancy. The details captured at each developmental stage of the unborn's life is intentionally outlined to create a visual and auditory image of the unborn's experience—*a vivid representation that will grip our consciences to revere the gift of life.*

FOREWORD
Jovia L. Godfrey

In May of 2005 I returned State-side from a semester overseas. Pregnant with ideations of my epic "Farewell Tour", I planned to spend the short Boston Summer with friends, family members, co-workers, and of course my boyfriend of four years. Things had been a bit rocky between us for some time, and we said we'd give it a real shot upon my arrival; but my 22-year-old mind believed that a final move to Spain would be just the "test" to be sure that our relationship could "make it." In hindsight, my plan was wholly self-motivated, and God exercised His rightful liberty to arrest my heart, mind, and actions for His purposes.

Six weeks into my "tour", my then boyfriend and I discovered that my ideations weren't the only thing that had been incubating. I was pregnant with our first child. To be clear, I do not pretend to understand God's ways around pregnancies and singleness. I do, however, believe in His sovereign power to give life as He sees fit. At the time, I was driven and ambitious (and arguably still am today); but there were some lessons on faith, patience, humility, power, diligence, and discernment that I am convinced I would never have learned to the degree that I have had it not been for the blessing of my desperate need for His guidance in raising His child. I would spend the subsequent years pouring over books, drinking in podcasts, and breathing the air of wisdom from dialogues with more seasoned women.

Chris and I continued to have four additional children... feeling, in a sense, that we had a secret to reveal: Babies do come with manuals.

The sharp hindsight of mothers and fathers before us... their writings and the richness of their time and energy spent with a young couple who at times didn't seem to get it... all this serves as our persistent guide, perpetual gifts, and a heritage of wholehearted, intentional, vulnerable parenting, which has, by God's grace bred whole, intentional, vulnerable children and young adults.

In the *God, Mommy, and Me* series, Dr. KB presents a manual, a guide, a gift, and a heritage for new parents today. What came to us in the early 2000s by way of desperate search and Divine answers, God has gifted to a generation who may find themselves ironically at risk of loss due to knowledge inundation.

Here are the thoughts, the words, and the prayers, packaged by the Author Himself, birthed through Dr. KB, and presented to you, mom... to you, dad... and to you, grandparents for your edification and for His glory.

I pray for clarity, discernment, and peace for you as the Holy Spirit guides you in His mission field of parenting with these texts in your heart.

TABLE OF CONTENTS

Week 1..1

Week 2..5

Week 3..9

Week 4...13

Week 5...17

Week 6...21

Week 7...25

Week 8...29

Week 9...33

Week 10..37

Week 11..41

Week 12..45

Week 13..49

Week 14..53

Week 15..57

Week 16..61

Week 17..65

Week 18..69

Week 19..73

Week 20..77

Week 21..81

Week 22..85

Week 23..89

Week 24..95

Week 25..99

Week 26..103

Week 27..107

Week 28..111

Week 29..115

Week 30..119

Week 31..123

Week 32..127

Week 33..133

Week 34..137

Week 35..143

Week 36..149

Week 37..153

Week 38..157

Week 39..163

Week 40..167

Week 41..171

Week 42..177

About The Book...183

WEEK 1

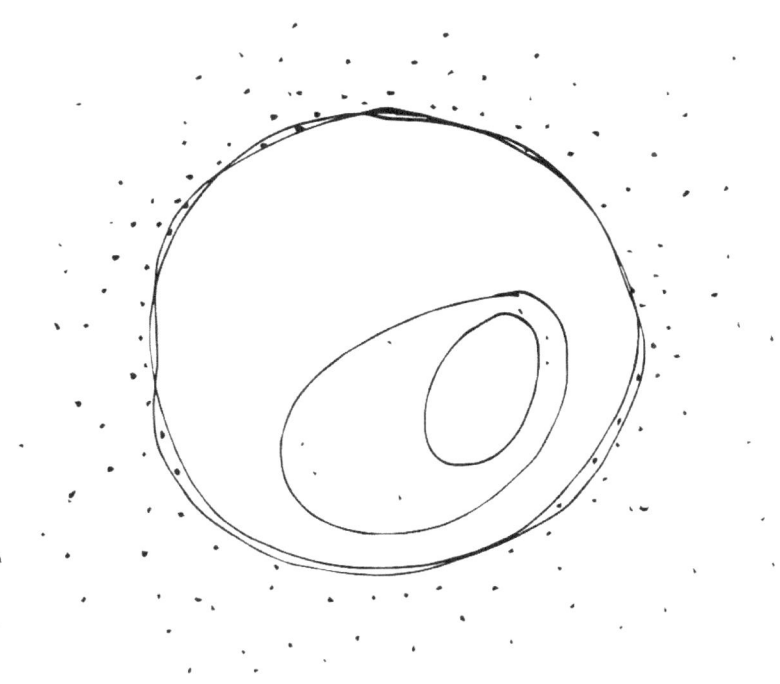

I am an oocyte.

Lo, children are an heritage of the Lord: and the fruit of the womb is his reward.

Psalm 127: 3 (KJV)

Dear Mom,

It may seem as if I am not present, but please do not ignore the fact that my *existence is* chronicled by a power that is greater than you and me. Look for me. Let the spirit of expectancy begin to rise within you. Your body is in preparation mode to receive me for I was sent to you and will reside in your womb. I will be housed in you and be nurtured by you. My entrance may be at an inopportune time, or maybe you have been waiting for this day. I am not sure how you feel about me but embrace this moment. In a few days or weeks, I will officially begin my journey with you.

Dear Child,

Are you there? I really do not know if I should celebrate. I know that there are a lot of hormonal changes occurring but right now, you are just a thought. I am not sure how things are going to happen, so I will just wait. I will start preparing to receive you. I will make great effort to prepare my mind, body and spirit so that I can care for you. I do not know much about you right now, but I do know that I am going to love you. I know that you and I will be a part of a divine plan, and I am ready. Let us hold each other's hand as He holds our hands. I will use this week to reflect on my thoughts and actions so that I can be aligned with heaven. I know we are going to embark on a journey that is so unique and yet divine. This week our *love-bond* starts, and I am excited, I am anxious, I am nervous, and I am happy. I am and I am………Oh my child, we are inseparable.

Dear Children,

You are a heritage of The Lord. You are of and from The Divine One. You belong to Him which makes you a part of the family and gives you rights to access Him. Your entrance into the human family was timely fashioned by The Godhead. You are not an accident. The beginning of this journey is the start of you spending time together with heaven. You cannot be separated from The Godhead. *"Where could I go from your Spirit? Or where could I flee from your presence? If I say, surely the darkness will overwhelm me. The light around me will be night, even the darkness doesn't hide from you, but the night shines as the day. The darkness is like light to you"* (Psalm 139:7 and 12, KJV). Take the time and sense your Heavenly Father's presence. As you witness the changes, take His hand and trust Him. He will never leave you or forsake you. Do not try to understand Him—**just TRUST Him**. Be fearless about who your Heavenly Father is and His unfailing love. Your confidence should not rest in your identity. This confidence in **self** is short-lived and at times self-gratifying. Rather, be confident in your Heavenly Father's identity. He is trustworthy. With Him, there is no fear. Start this journey with a measure of assurance that He is dependable. *"Being confident of this very thing, that he which hath begun a good work in you will perform it………..."* (Philippians 1:6-7a, KJV).

WEEK 2

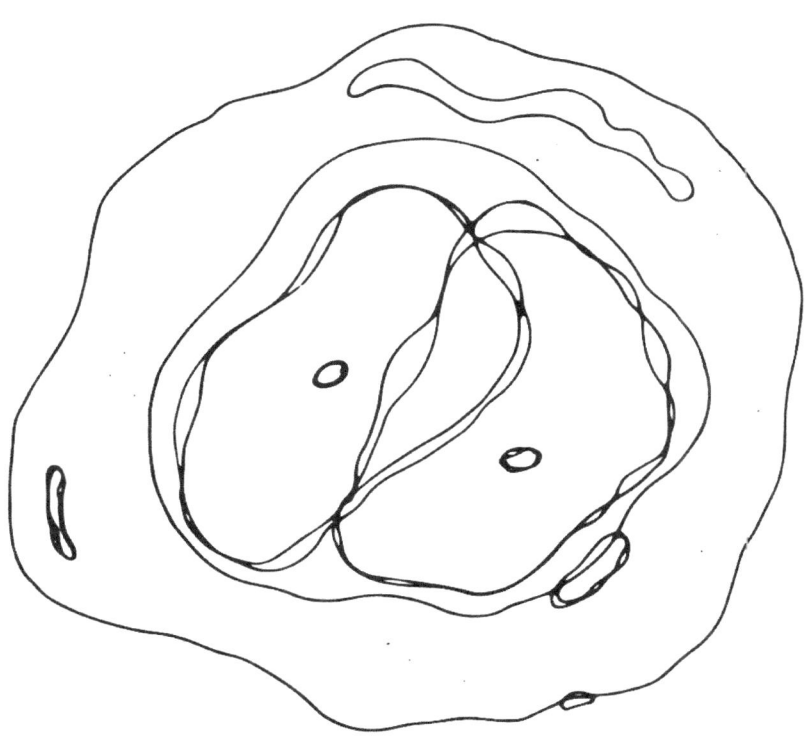

I am going through mitosis.

Then the word of the Lord came unto me, saying, Before I formed thee in the belly I knew thee; and before thou camest forth out of the womb I sanctified thee, and I ordained thee a prophet unto the nations.

Jeremiah 1: 4-5 (KJV)

Dear Mom,

The complexities and the intricate details of my journey are not fully understood. This week your hormones are completely under my influence. You may feel irritable, cranky, overly emotional or 'unpregnant'. Some doctors still believe that you are not officially pregnant, yet this week is vital in our story. I need you Mom to be intentional in your habits and adjust your lifestyle to embrace my delicate entrance. Consider this week's unfolding as a piece of the puzzle. It is amazing that my genetic coding is going to be embodied in a single cell that your body will release. What a master plan!

Dear Child,

Oh, my dear child I want to be excited, but it is too early to put my dancing shoes on. The only sign I have that you are possibly here is that I am having symptoms of ovulation. The journey is so early, but there is a lot I can do. I will start taking my prenatal vitamins and I will start getting my womb ready to carry you inside of me. It is so early to even think about who you are or who you will become. I cannot help myself....It is never too early to start loving you. The Divine One is so concerned about every detail. He is still polishing the intricacies of our time together. Oh, what wonderful love. You and I will be a part of a masterpiece, a work of art and a holy moment.

Dear Children,

Before you were formed in the belly, your God, your Father, your Papa knew you. He is not surprised by your existence. You may and will not understand the intricacies of this experience. If God should unveil the intricacies of this experience, it would boggle your mind. Rest assured that He is with you. A masterpiece design is about to unfold. You will become more aware that you are not here by chance. Your Father knows YOU and He has called you by your name. "*Because thou hast made the Lord, which is my refuge, even the most High, thy habitation; There shall no evil befall thee, neither shall any plague come nigh thy dwelling.............Because he hath set his love upon me, therefore will I deliver him: I will set him on high, because he hath known my name. He shall call upon me, and I will answer him: I will be with him in trouble; I will deliver him, and honor him. With long life will I satisfy him, and shew him my salvation"* (Psalm 91: 9-10 and 14-16, KJV). Have confidence in your Heavenly Father's sovereignty. Before the world came into existence, He was and still IS.

WEEK 3

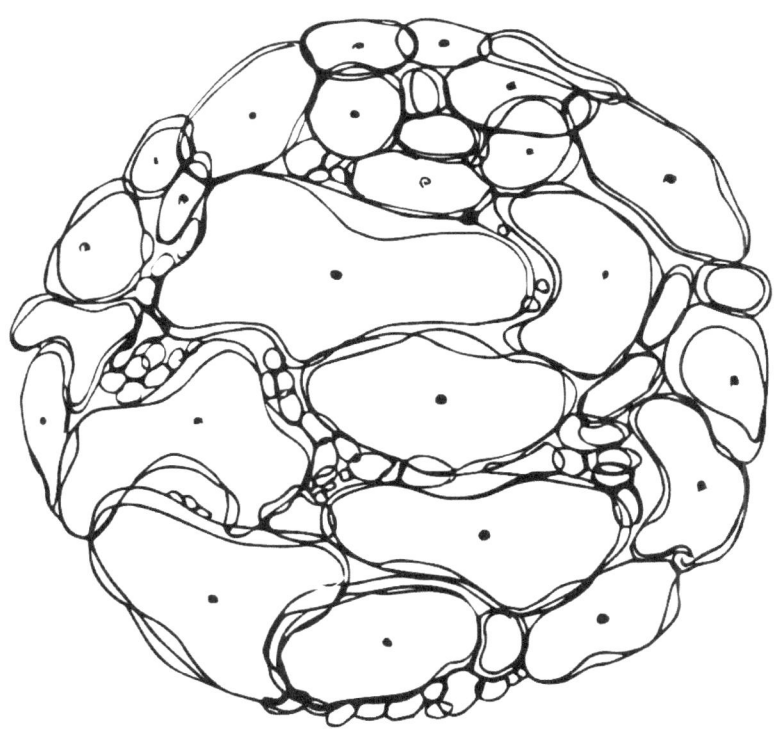

I am a blastocyst.

Are not five sparrows sold for two farthings, and not one of them is forgotten before God?

Luke 12: 6, KJV.

Dear Mom,

My substance has been formed; the sperm and the egg have been fused together. I am deep within your fallopian tubes. I exist at a microscopic level, but I am here. This part of our journey cannot be erased. Oh Mom! If you could see the intricacies of fertilization- your egg has even built a protective wall to prevent other sperms from entering its space. What a beauty in creation! By the way, they have given me a name—*I have been called a zygote but will later turn into a blastocyst.* Yippee!! In a short time, I will be fully a part of your world. It is amazing to be the embodiment of approximately 60 cells that have been coded to perform an exact function. Mom, a master designer knows every cell of my being!

Dear Child,

Yippee. Congratulations, we are now officially a team. Our love bond has begun. I am 'pregnantish' and one or more of my eggs has/have been fertilized. I have not yet started feeling the effects of pregnancy hormones, but I am supposed to be pregnant. I heard it is still too early for me to know that I am pregnant. This is new for me, and I feel a little anxious because I do not know the details of my journey. I do not know if I am going to be sick or not. Either way I know I am going to love you. It is amazing the love between a mom and her baby— ***she will do anything for that child that she carries inside.*** I know that He who has begun a work inside of me will give me the grace to endure every challenge that will come with this journey. My sweetheart, we are in this together and He has etched you on the palm of His hands.

Dear Children,

What a sacred truth that you are not forgotten. How could the master designer forget that He has orchestrated your existence and the plans for your life? You are worth so much more than you can ever imagine. The birds, animals, and even the tiniest creatures confidently move about because they know that the master designer is trustworthy. Then, why do you fear? He is with you, and He is your father. Rest………you are not interrupting His God-time. He is delighted to be with you. Each cell has been created by your Heavenly Father. The mitochondria, the cytoplasm, the nucleus, the cytoskeleton……. all reflect His glory. Your Heavenly

Father has taken great care to ensure that each detail is perfectly in sync. **YOU ARE HIS**. *"Put not your trust in princes, nor in the son of man, in whom there is no help. Happy is he that hath the God of Jacob for his help, whose hope is in the Lord his God: Which made heaven, and earth, the sea, and all that therein is: which keepeth truth for ever"* (Psalm 146: 3, 5-6, KJV). This declaration echoes full coverage for humanity and the entire universe. You are a part of *"........whose hope is in the Lord his God: Which made heaven, and earth, the sea,* **and ALL that therein is**............*"*.

WEEK 4

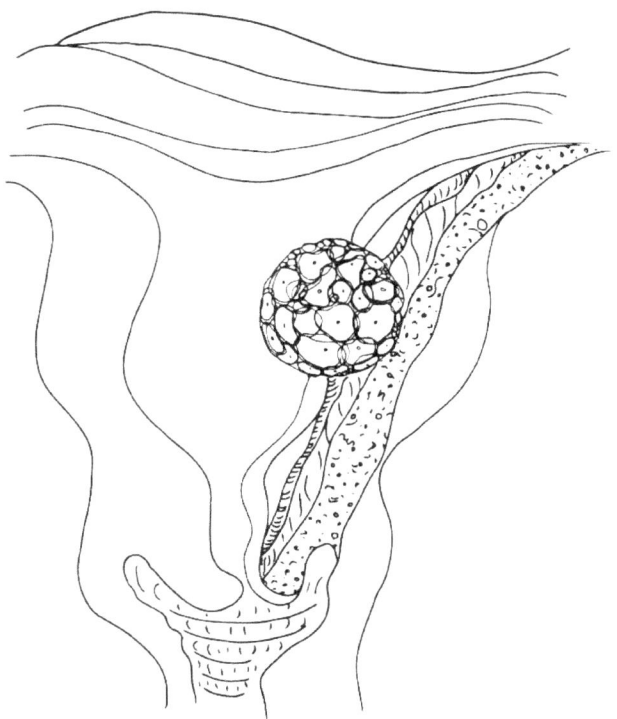

Implantation stage: I am about the size of a poppy seed.

0.04in/0.10cm long

*For thou hast possessed my reins:
thou hast covered me in my
mother's womb.*

Psalm 139: 13

Dear Mom,

I am now a blastocyst, and I am ready to be implanted. By divine orchestration I will be living in you for an extended time. I am not sure if you felt me embedding myself in you. Either way....*I am here.* This week I am the size of a poppy seed, and I am barely visible to the naked eye, but I am here. There is a lot of cell separation that is going on, and the cells are forming different layers. There are three different layers of cells working together. The outer layer will eventually form my skin. The middle layer will form my muscles, and the inner layer will form my internal organs. I am just a whole bunch of cells coming together, and I am being programmed to grow inside of you. Mom, if you do a pregnancy test, I bet that I will show up. Can I start calling you Mom? I can already feel the bond between you and me.

Dear Child,

This week is the '**Big I**' Week- **I**mplantation week. Our journey has begun! I am not sure of the intricacies, but you have found a way down to my uterus and made a comfortable place to nestle yourself for the next 36 weeks or more. I am sure that our journey has begun because I missed my menstrual cycle this week. I also feel some fullness in my lower pelvic area. First, I thought it was gas or maybe I was just bloated, but then after eating, I realized that the feeling was still there. Although I missed my menstrual cycle, I am still checking every minute to make sure that my menstrual cycle is not going to be here this month. It feels like I have been waiting for eternity. I am kind of feeling over emotional, a little bit moody, a little bit groggy and at the same time very apprehensive. What is really going on inside of me? I really do not know and I want to know. Little one, are you there?

Dear Children,

You have been covered in your mother's womb. The details of your life are perfectly planned. Your journey has been mapped. Turn on your GPS—**G**od **P**resence **S**ystem. As the journey unfolds- trust that I AM is more than able. In your time zone, this journey is marked by days/weeks/months/trimesters. However, in your Heavenly Father's space, there is NO time. His sovereignty is not bound by time. This journey is sacred!

His presence will cover you. You are enveloped by a divine presence. The **I Am** is GOD! He is present.

*"**I am** the bread of life"* (John 6:35, KJV).

*"**I am** the light of the world"* (John 8:12, KJV).

*"**I am** the good shepherd"* (John 10:11, KJV).

*"**I am** the way, the truth, and the life"* (John 14:6, KJV).

*"**I am** the true vine"* (John 15:1, KJV).

*"**I am** the resurrection and the life"* (John 11:25, KJV).

Is there anything to fear with this blank check that the **I AM** has handed to you? *"And this is the confidence that we have in him, that, if we ask anything according to his will, he heareth us: And if we know that he hears us, whatsoever we ask, we know that we have the petitions that we desired of him"* (1 John 5: 14-15, KJV). You have just unlocked heaven's treasures and unleashed your Heavenly Father's goodness in your life. Use this journey to restore your faith in His word. Indeed, the **I AM** is here, with and in you.

WEEK 5

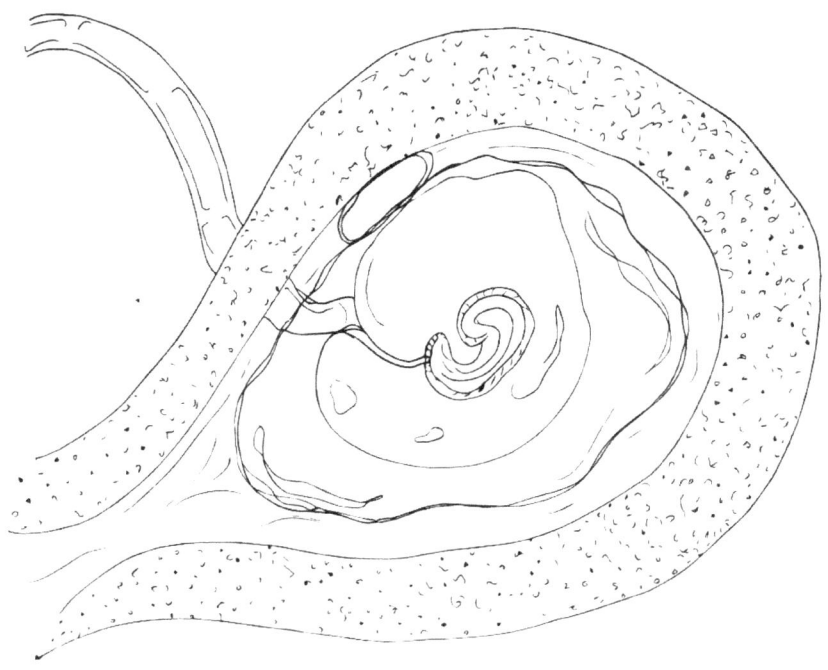

I am about the size of an American apple seed.

0.05in/0.12cm long

*I will praise thee; for I am
fearfully and wonderfully made:
marvelous are thy works; and
that my soul knoweth right well.*

Psalm 139: 14

Dear Mom,

I know you are getting suspicious that something strange is happening inside you. You may be feeling lightheaded, queasy, lethargic or even a bit weak. All those feelings are because of me. The great news is that the countdown has officially begun, and we are on the growth clock. This week is so special to my growth since the placenta and amniotic sac are forming and my little heart has started to beat and send blood throughout my tiny body. Oh mom…...even my brain and spinal cord are forming. I know that as I grow all my organs will eventually look different- right now they are perfectly filled with life.

Dear Child,

Little one, oh my little one I am beginning to get very suspicious that there is something growing on the inside of me. I am not quite sure if it is you, but I feel somewhat different than my usual self. Should I go see a doctor right now? Or maybe I could just do one of those home pregnancy testing kits. It is too early to start telling family and friends that I think I am 'pregnantish'. So, I think I am going to wait. In the meantime, I am beginning to get very cautious about my food choices, and even with medication, I am starting to second-guess what is safe. I want to do everything that I can to make sure you are healthy and strong. I am starting to feel kind of tired, and my breasts are tender. I guess this is normal when you are 'pregnantish'.

Dear Children,

You are fearfully and wonderfully made. As this journey unfolds, praise and adoration must freely flow from your lips. As this beautiful creature is being formed, you will begin to hear His *God-whispers*. Each day you will learn how to sense His presence. He is not loud, nor does He yell for your attention. Remove yourself from the noise of your life and hear His whispers. This journey requires only one director and that is your Heavenly Father. There will be days when you feel as if everything is out of control. Trust His words and rest assured that those are the days when He is in total control. Whenever you feel the need to take the reins of this journey, remember that He has already appointed this moment for you. His control is not to hinder you from being you. He is simply trying to guide your footsteps in the right path—**a path that benefits you**. Be still. This journey has just started and yet, our Heavenly Father already knows the outcome. Your Heavenly Father is already in your future. Embrace each moment. He is the Alpha and the Omega—the Beginning and the End. "*O taste and see that the Lord is good: blessed is the man that trusteth in him. O fear the Lord, ye his saints: for there is no want to them that fear him*" (Psalm 34: 8-9, KJV).

WEEK 6

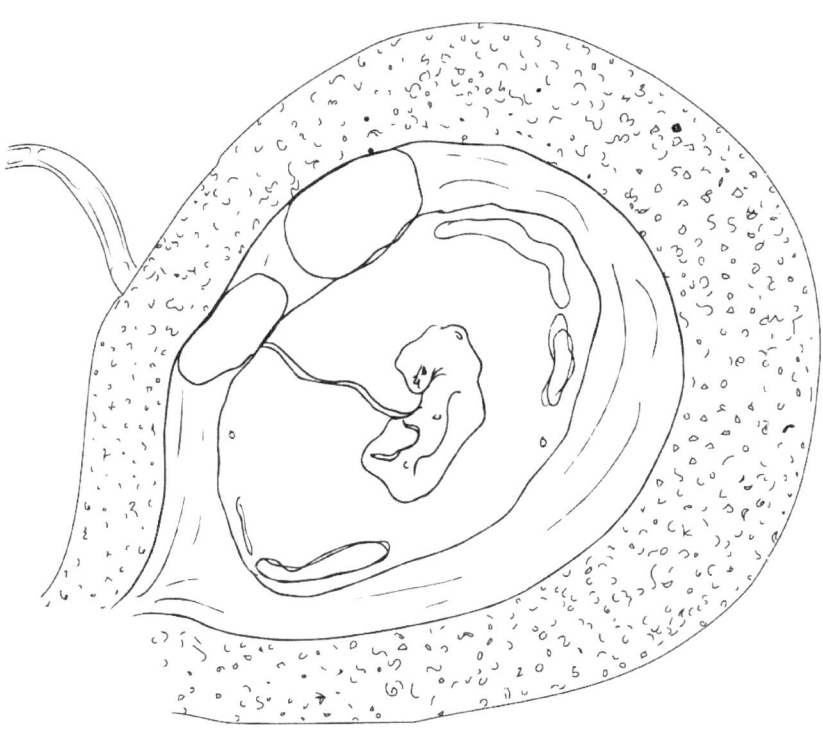

I am about the size of a pomegranate seed.

0.13in/0.5cm long

*For I know the thoughts that
I think toward you, saith the
Lord, thoughts of peace, and not
of evil, to give you an expected
end.*

Jeremiah 29: 11

Dear Mom,

My photo shoots are not cute right now. When compared to my body, my head is very large and there are folds. Not to worry, what you see will eventually form my face and my cheeks. You should also see Mom, on either side of my body there are also bud-like lumps. Relax Mom, the buds will morph into my arms and legs. My ear canals are also in the early stage of formation. Right now, I cannot hear your voice, but I can feel your undying love for me. Oh Mom, I cannot wait to see your beautiful face.

Dear Child,

The hormones in my body are shifting!!!!! I am not 100% sure but I am making lifestyle changes to protect you. I cannot wait to tell everyone about you. I am kind of anxious because I need to know for sure. Either way, I have been chosen to embark on a journey with heaven. Your existence is heaven and earth coming together as one, and we are a part of this moment. It is early days, but I am embracing this life that is growing inside me. The details of this phase are not fully known to humanity, but we are entering a territory that is completely controlled by divinity.

Dear Children,

When your Heavenly Father thinks about you, He thinks of peace and a wonderful end. If only you could see the thoughts He has towards you. His plans for you are absolutely good. He is your Heavenly Father and He is concerned about your life. He is forever committed to caring for you. Take refuge in His words. He is a God that cannot lie. He is True and Faithful. Your world is perhaps filled with instability, but that does not affect His *God-ability*. He is immutable therefore He cannot change. He is the one constant in your life. Recommit your thoughts and your ways to The Holy One. Let Him be the focal place of your thoughts. Oh, gaze upon His face. Let His love caress your worrisome spirit. As this journey unfolds in front of you, relinquish your desire to fixate your mind on the '*what ifs.*' These prolonged thoughts on the uncertainties of this journey can cripple your faith. It is human to get flustered about the future, especially when there is not a script that maps out the plans. He understands your worries but if you let your worries go untamed, they will disable your trust. When your intense *what-ifs* seek to overwhelm you, quickly dismiss the urge to dwell in the unknown. Heaven has already decided that all is well. *"Casting all your care upon him; for he careth for you"* (1 Peter 5:7, KJV). Your *what ifs* are fears in disguise. They are dark forces that will attach to your spirit and unravel your theology. Cut the umbilical cord of fear. Do not feed it. Do not nourish it. Fear is a direct connection to the devil- the enemy of your soul. This enemy knows that fear will dismantle the core of your soul. *"Neither give place to the devil"* (Ephesians 4: 27, KJV). Do not embrace the pseudo packages of fear—phobia, anxiety, stress, concern, panic, hyperventilation, alarm, trepidation, or dismay. These softer tones that are wrapped and tied with a bow, are no less potent than the blatant word called FEAR. Your Heavenly Father knows the plans that He has for you, and it is the mission of the evil one to get you to not believe that your Heavenly Father is credible. Trust your Papa! Trust your Heavenly Father.

WEEK 7

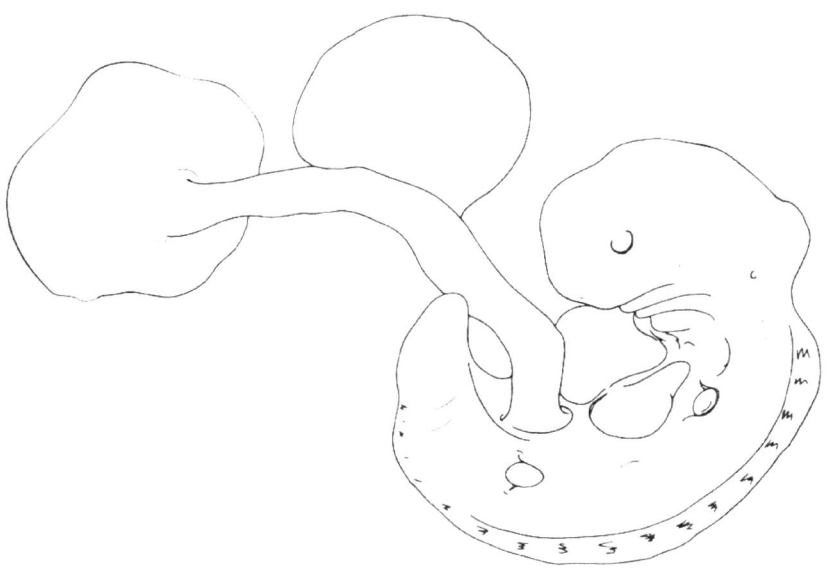

I am about the size of a small blueberry.

0.37in/0.95cm long

My substance was not hidden from thee, when I was made in secret, and curiously wrought in the lowest parts of the earth.

Psalm 139: 15

Dear Mom,

We are halfway through the first trimester, and I am about the size of a small blueberry. Your womb is growing bigger to accommodate my growth and for that I will always be grateful. I am still very small and so you might not be able to feel me moving inside of you. But hold a minute! The doctor said that I have grown 10,000 times more than when you conceived. It is now my seventh week living inside of you and I am loving every minute of it! I love you so much mom. I just love calling your name.........***Mom***.

Dear Child,

This week I am officially a little halfway through the first trimester. There is not a lot of visible evidence that you are here but be assured that there are changes underway inside your little house. I heard that you are just like a small raspberry or a blueberry (yum). By the way, you are tiny, but you are already growing into a wonderful being that I will truly love. I am already making plans to cherish each moment that I will have with you. I am taking one day at a time, but my stomach is filled with wonders. It is queasy, unsettled, strange…. I do not know how I should describe my feelings. Being your mom is starting to be my focus. Many months are ahead of us, and we are yet to discover the full plan of the master designer.

Dear Children,

There was no secret when you were formed. Your very existence is not a surprise to The Master designer. His eyes saw you. His eyes will continue to see you. Every cell, nerve, tissue, organ, and body system have been fashioned by your Heavenly Father. He is God and there is no one that can be compared to Him. He did not take counsel when He was making you. All the details of your being start and finish with Him. You are valuable to your Heavenly Father. You are worth everything to Him, including him giving His son's life for you. You are worth everything, that He was willing to leave the throne room and step down into the muck of humanity. There is nothing that you can ever do that would make your Heavenly Father love you less and there is nothing you could ever do to make Him love you more. He loves you with an everlasting love. *"Be strong and of a good courage, fear not, nor be afraid of them: for the Lord thy God, he it is that doth go with thee; he will not fail thee, nor forsake thee"* (Deuteronomy 31:

6, KJV). Feel the kiss of heaven's bliss in this precious and sacred moment. Heaven rejoices over this created life. Listen…... the angels are rejoicing over you. Relax. Trust Him. *"And the Lord, he it is that doth go before thee; he will be with thee, he will not fail thee, neither forsake thee: fear not, neither be dismayed"* (Deuteronomy 31: 8, KJV).

WEEK 8

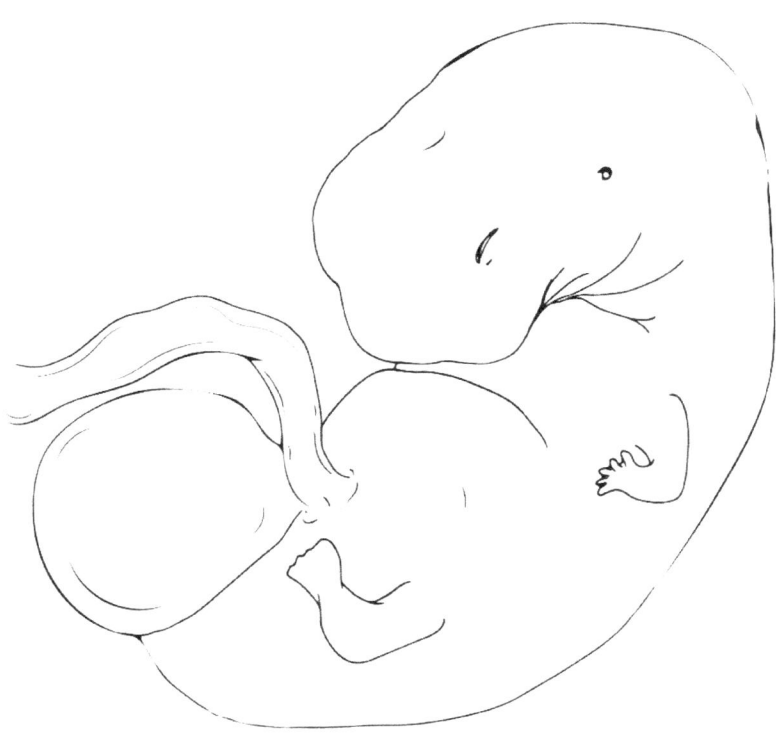

I am about the size of a small raspberry.

0.63in/1.6cm long

Thine eyes did see my substance, yet being unperfect and in thy book all my members were written, which in continuance were fashioned, when as yet there was none of them.

Psalm 139: 16

Dear Mom,

My first trimester is almost nearing the end. It may seem as if we just started and there is not much development that is accomplished, but that is not true. I am almost at the stage when I will be declared a fetus. I am less than half an inch long and I am going to lose my tail-like features in just a few hours. My head is still big, and my body is still tiny, and I am so not ready for a photoshoot. However, my fingers, legs, lips, and toes are getting defined. Mom oh Mom, the valves of my heart which will send air to my lungs are formed. Mom, Mom, Mom!!!!!!!!! My bones have started to come alive, and I can bend my elbows and wrist. Yippee!!!

Dear Child,

This is a big week, and I have four more weeks before I can officially say the first trimester has ended. I am feeling a sense that this journey is going to require faith. I am lessening my focus on the physiological changes that are happening to me and zeroing in on my role in this masterpiece plan. You and I are walking a path which requires me to trust the unknown. When there was none of you or me, there was The Divine One- The Holy One of Israel. How can He know YOU and you are not even fully formed? Why do you matter to Him when you are little more than a microscopic being? *"For thou hast possessed my reins: thou hast covered me in my mother's womb. I will praise thee; for I am fearfully and wonderfully made: marvellous are thy works; and that my soul knoweth right well. My substance was not hid from thee, when I was made in secret, and curiously wrought in the lowest parts of the earth. Thine eyes did see my substance, yet being unperfect; and in thy book all my members were written, which in continuance were fashioned, when as yet there was none of them. How precious also are thy thoughts unto me, O God! how great is the sum of them!" Psalm 139: 13-17,* KJV).

Dear Children,

He saw you in your uncomely state and He loved you then and He loves you now. You are blessed. All things belong to your Heavenly Father. He is your father and all that He has makes you an heir to His kingdom. His presence fills the universe. As you move about, and as you take this journey of faith, realize that you are truly blessed. He will direct your steps- ***just trust Him***. Your Heavenly Father will order every move you make—***just***

trust Him. Give your worries and your burdens to Him. *"The Holy One will give unto them beauty for ashes, the oil of joy for mourning, the garment of praise for the spirit of heaviness; that they might be called trees of righteousness, the planting of the Lord, that he might be glorified"* (Isaiah 61: 3, KJV). This journey is your moment to come in alignment with Heaven. Experience a slice of divine greatness. You will receive double for all of the challenges you face. Everlasting joy shall be yours. Rebuke every negative thought that is not in line with what your Heavenly Father says about you. Forsake every habit that works against your Heavenly Father's will for your life. Begin to accept that God is delighted that you are His child. Believing that God is for you and not against you is not enough. You need to now accept and believe. You are loved by your Heavenly Father!

WEEK 9

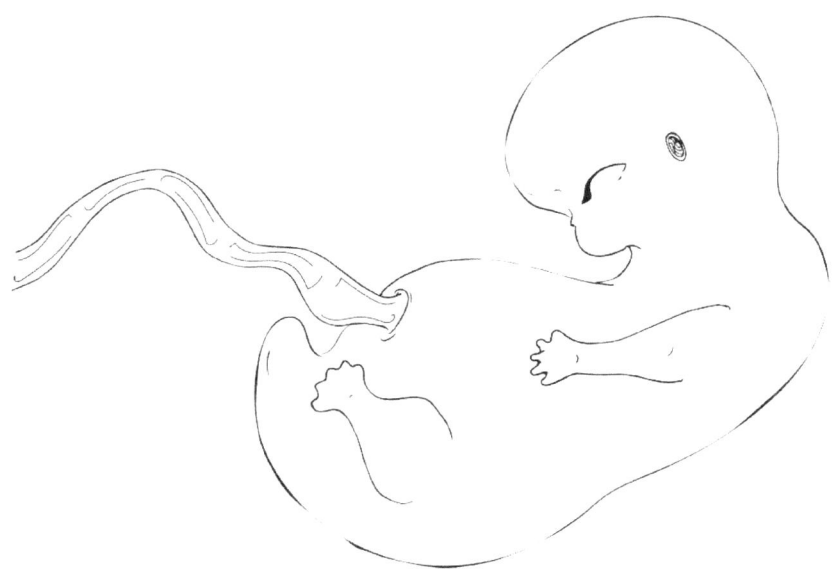

I am about the size of a cherry.

0.9in/2.3cm long

Thou hast clothed me with skin and flesh, and hast fenced me with bones and sinews.

Job 10: 11

Dear Mom,

I am 1 inch long and I love the length of my body. On average, I am about the size of a cherry. My eyes are growing bigger, and my ears are becoming fully defined inside and out. I now have an extremely tiny tongue, and I am getting used to my tooth buds. I am not the only one changing, because you are also seeing changes in your body. Your cute little pants may not be so cute anymore. There are bulges everywhere on your body and you may be seeing blotches and blemishes all over your body. Please do not get upset. It is a part of our growing pains. We will get through this together. We are a family…. *Are we not mom?*

Dear Child,

I stand in awe at the greatness of God and His keen attention to the smallest details of my life. I am officially in the last week of my first trimester and there are good days and there are days when I do not feel so 'peachy'. However, you are here and there is a sudden reality that I am responsible for someone else. I am becoming less worried about myself, and I am learning to think outside of my ME world. Each day I sense the urge to find the answers to my *whys*. Why was I chosen to partner with heaven? Do I really meet the qualifications of a God who knows the real me? Am I worthy of being your mother? Then there are deeper questions of my capacity to be your mother. My questions are haunting me and yet there is a whisper of my Heavenly Father's voice reassuring me that my questions have already been answered and my battles have already been won. Both you and I are His! We are a part of His orchestrated plan. *"Are not five sparrows sold for two farthings, and not one of them is forgotten before God? But even the very hairs of your head are all numbered. Fear not therefore: ye are of more value than many sparrows"* (Luke 12: 6-7, KJV).

Dear Children,

Your Heavenly Father crafted you in His glory. Like as He did to the first man Adam, He did to you. He formed him and then breathed into his nostrils, and he became a living soul. Oh, that you would see the intricacies of your existence. You were timely fashioned into an instrument that met your Heavenly Father's approval. After each day of creation, He looked and said *it was good*. He is looking at you at this moment, and He has declared that YOU are good. Your body is a vehicle for His presence. You are worth every minute of His creative power. You did not happen by chance. *"And God said, Let us make man in our image, after our likeness:......"* (Genesis 1: 26a, KJV). If you could see The Godhead at work in this journey, you would begin to understand the details of your Heavenly Father's handiwork. *"So God created man in his own image, in the image of God created he him;......."* (Genesis 1: 27a, KJV). His **God-power** is fully active when a soul is created. He pays attention to your wellbeing. If He takes the time to care about the existence of a wild animal, why would He then create you and leave you to figure things out on your own? He has created you just a little lower than the angels. The Godhead has downloaded in you to a lesser degree comparative power to the angels. Dominion of the earth has been placed in mankind's care. It was His intention for humanity to have full authority over the earth. He has not diminished mankind's capabilities of greatness. As you move into your different spaces, reflect on the authority that was bestowed upon you. Your existence is deliberately interjected in this earth. You have been given His stamp of approval.

WEEK 10

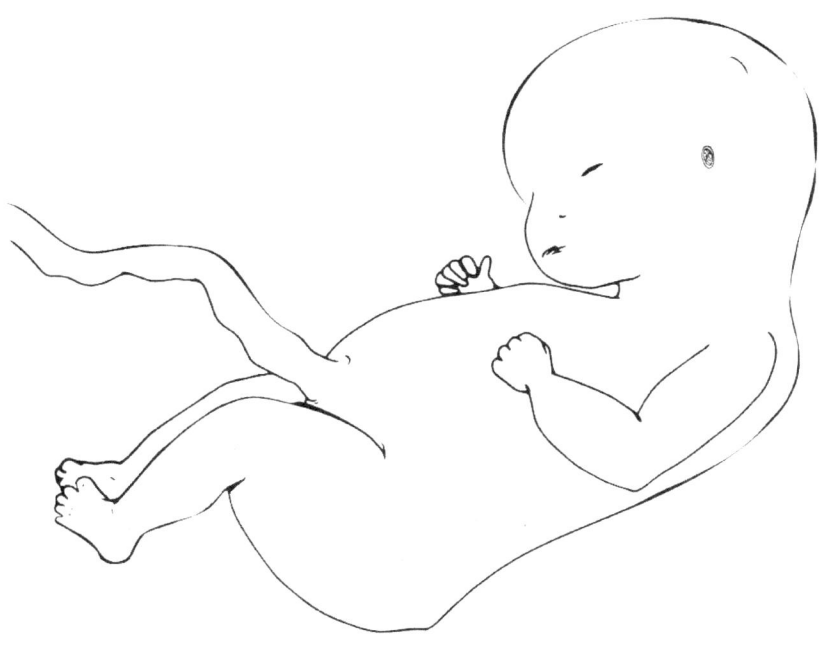

Fetal Stage: I am about the size of a kumquat.

1.22in/3.1cm long

The spirit of God hath made me, and the breath of the Almighty hath given me life.

Job 33: 4

Dear Mom,

This week I am a miniature version of what I will be when I am born-only much smaller. Oh Mom, please make sure you are eating all of your green leafy vegetables. I know they are bland, and they might not be your favorite, but I am really going to need them so that my organs can be properly developed. It is too early to call it……. but this week I am getting toenails and fingernails, *but they are not quite ready for a pedicure and a manicure* (laugh out loud). I am still a tiny person, but my kidneys are starting to filter their blood, and it is also making urine. That is not all that is happening this week. I am also having digestive juices in my stomach. My head is still large when compared to the rest of my body, but my neck and all of the bones in my face are fully formed. **I am fully human**. I even have fine hair covering my body and my eyes are fully developed. I cannot wait to see your face and hear your voice and touch you. I love you so much…. I am yours, Mom.

Dear Child,

To think that almost all your organs are formed by the tenth week is beyond my feeble imagination. It is even more unfathomable to think that you are a miniature version of how you will be at birth. This is a masterpiece of intricacies crafted by a divine hand. Hanby the songwriter echoes the words *"Who is He in yonder stall, at whose feet the shepherds fall? Tis the Lord, O wondrous story! Tis the Lord, the King of glory! At His feet we humbly fall, Crown Him, crown Him Lord of all!"* Oh, my baby, my child, you are a wonder of His creation. You are beautiful.

Dear Children,

God has the authority over life, and He has chosen to give you life. In real time, God's breath is in you. It takes the divine action of God for you to breathe. Your existence is not by accident. You being alive did not occur by a mere lottery play by the Almighty God. This reality should motivate you to recognize that carrying a baby is a holy moment in time. You were chosen to carry a breathing human inside of you. This *God-decision* conveys that you have met His approval to be a part of His divine orchestrated plans. Do not take for granted this act of God. He is all powerful and yet He is concerned with the little details of your existence. *"Thine, O Lord is the greatness, and the power, and the glory, and the victory, and the majesty: for all that is in the heaven and in the earth is thine; thine is the kingdom, O Lord, and thou art exalted as head above all"* (1 Chronicles 29:11, KJV). Resist the desire to linger your mind on future worries. This desire oftentimes results in a surge of fear. If God's breath is residing in you, it means that your tomorrows are in His control. Fear is tormenting and has the capacity to disrupt your faith. Revere this journey in light of the fact that God has chosen to include you in His plan to breathe His spirit and make a living soul. He may not reveal all His plans for this journey and beyond, so rest……. Breathe. His breath— ***it is a gift from the Holy One.***

WEEK 11

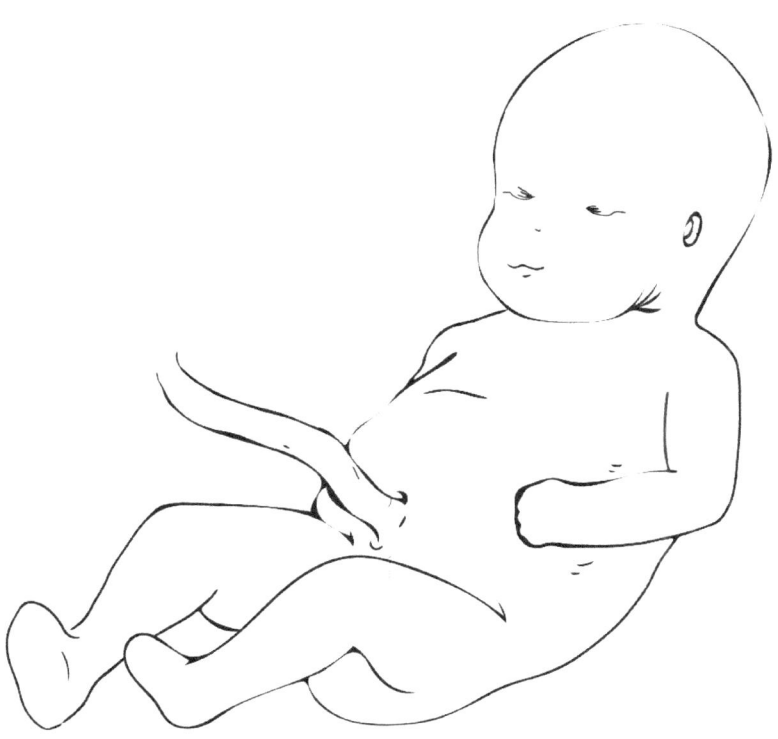

I am about the size of a lime.

1.61in/4.1cm long

And he will love thee, and bless thee, and multiply thee: he will also bless the fruit of thy womb

Deuteronomy 7: 13

Dear Mom,

You are almost a third of your way through the pregnancy journey. We are ending our first trimester together. Almost! I am still tiny, but I am almost 2 inches long. I am definitely a miniature version of me—*the me at birth*. I am the size of a lime, and I am sure you are now conscious of my presence in your womb. Your bladder is fuller. You are eating more food, and you are beginning to sense and to feel me. My forehead is less bulging, and my eyes are now right in the middle of my face. I now have digits which are toes and fingers, and they are no longer looking like webbed feet. My external genitals are also forming, even though they are tiny. You can now start to think if I am going to be a girl or am I going to be a boy. Things are moving faster even though you are moving slower. No worries. It is because I am getting bigger and I guess you are getting bigger too. I still think you are beautiful… Mom.

Dear Child,

How much more love can a mother feel for a child she has not met? Every day when I am awake, I find myself thinking about you. I imagine holding you in my arms and wishing that everything is going to be perfect. But the truth is I do not know what the future holds for both of us. I only know that our master designer is already in all of our tomorrows. You are blessed! *"God is not a man, that he should lie; neither the son of man, that he should repent: hath he said, and shall he not do it? or hath he spoken, and shall he not make it good?"* (Numbers 23: 19, KJV).

Dear Children,

God has blessed you and you will operate in abundance and overflow. He has crowned you with glory and honor. A word has been released from the mouth of God and that is - *He will bless and multiply you and He will also bless the fruit of your womb.* His words did not convey a suggestion. He is a God that cannot tell a lie. If you are concerned that you are not a part of the outpouring of His blessing, at least appreciate the fact that the fruit of your womb is a direct recipient of His blessings. The wavering of your faith is not related to God's character. His desire to bless the fruit of your womb is not negotiable. Oh, that God's children would sense His desire to lavish His children with His multiplicative blessings. He will bless you, but He is longing to do an ***ALSO-blessing of your offspring***. God wants to do an expanded blessing. That means you and the child that you are carrying are existing under an open-heaven blessing. Change your mindset about the dependency model of blessing—**if** you do this, **then** I will do that. God has an unbreakable covenant with His children. He cannot recall his words. There is a lifetime warranty on His promises. He has promised that He will LOVE you, BLESS you, MULTIPLY you, and BLESS your offspring. *"Now unto him that is able to do exceeding abundantly above all that we ask or think,......"* (Ephesians 3: 20a, KJV).

WEEK 12

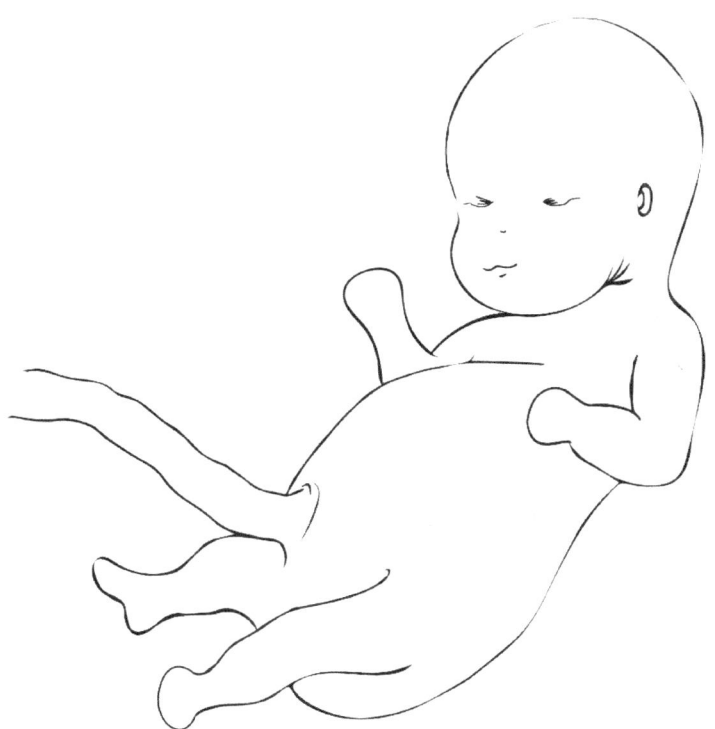

I am about the size of a plum.

2.13in/5.4cm long

But even the very hairs of your head are all numbered. Fear not therefore: ye are of more value than many sparrows.

Luke 12: 7

Dear Mom,

You can breathe a sigh of relief, mom. We just made it to the end of one of the most challenging times of our lives- *the end of the first trimester*. Make sure you are doing a lot of deep breathing. I know the pressure of me being in this cozy little house of yours aka (also known as) the womb is placing pressure on your lungs. It seems you can hardly breathe. But no worries, we have some more weeks together and it is worth every minute of this extra pressure. I am twice the size I was 3 weeks ago. I am the size of a plum- which is about 2 to 2 and one-half inches long. I am beginning to move all the time. I am kicking. I am stretching. I am turning. I am rolling. I am twisting. You may not feel all what I am doing, but I am moving, and I am pressing against your uterine wall. Guess what Mom? **I can suck my thumb**. My intestines are contracting and relaxing and I am beginning to poop. Yuck. No worries. It is not too yucky. I am growing and getting bigger every day. By the way, I cannot promise you that this pooping thing is over. I heard there is a lot more where this one came from. Laugh out loud!

Dear Child,

How can another human come from another human? How can a microscopic thing become a fully grown being? These are some of my questions and I am not sure if I want the answers. Not knowing everything increases my trust and I am okay with total reliance. I am using this journey to reaffirm my awareness of God's presence. I will not require Him to answer these questions, just as I have never asked the pilot to confirm his aviation credentials. I simply sit on the aircraft and trust the pilot's capabilities. Then why should I ask our Heavenly Father, the master designer, to answer my wonderings? Isn't He credible? My child, let us relax and take this journey one day at a time.

Dear Children,

This journey is a team effort that requires earth to work directly with heaven. God knows exactly what is required for this experience to leave you standing in awe. This experience is training you to fully place your existence in God's care. He will listen to your voice and attentively respond to your every need. He might not answer your requests exactly the way you want, but trust that He knows what is best for your life. He is not a God that takes pleasure in seeing His children hurting. So everyday tastes of the multitude of His mercies. Put your trust in Him. Be joyful for He has surrounded you with His favor. *"These things have I spoken unto you, that my joy might remain in you, and that your joy might be full"* (St. John 15: 11, KJV). He has made a covenant with you that He will never leave you or forsake you. Your Heavenly Father will be here to comfort you in times when you feel overwhelmed with the changes. Place your attention on Him and the rapid changes that are occurring in you will diminish in His presence. As you become more aware of the peace that you can find in your Heavenly Father's presence, you will experience a calm. Put your confidence in the Holy One. He has never forsaken anyone who trusted in Him. In His presence there is complete joy, and He wants to lavish you with His joy.

WEEK 13

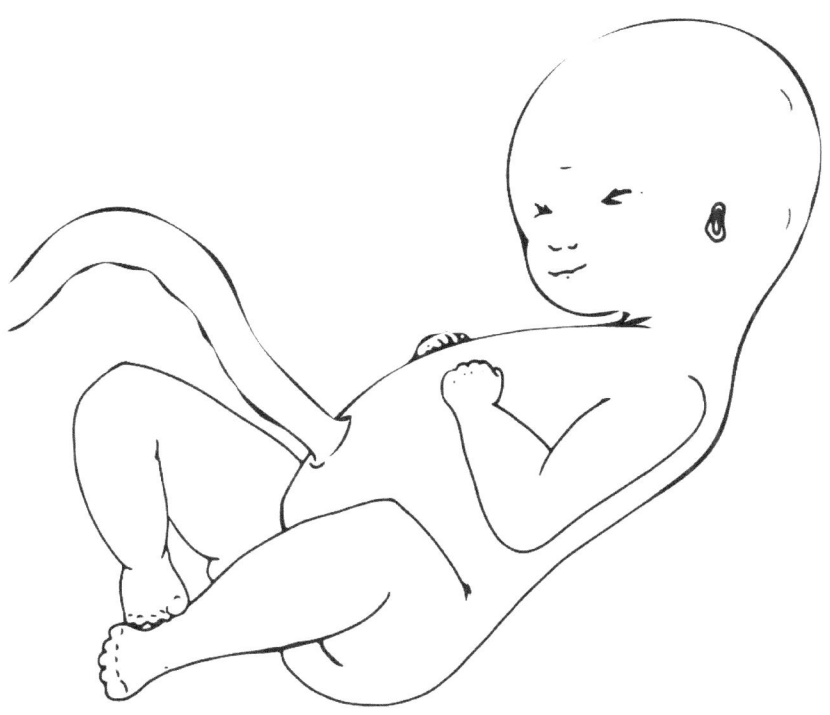

I am about the size of a lemon.

2.19in/7.4cm long

The Lord will perfect that which concerneth me: thy mercy, O Lord, endureth for ever: forsake not the works of thine own hands.

Psalm 138: 8

Dear Mom,

Hopefully you are feeling better this week. Maybe you are thinking that pregnancy is not so crappy after all. At least I hope so because I love living inside of you. By now, if you went to the doctor, you should have heard my heartbeat. Boom-boom-boom. I am alive Mom! I know that this week you are starting to feel as if you are eating for two and you may be gaining weight for two. But remember, it is not the quantity of food you eat, but it is the quality of food. So be careful that you do not put on those extra pounds; but if you do, you are still my mom.

Dear Child,

I have found a way to be at peace with this journey. It is the type of peace that comes from knowing that I am not in control nor can I control the unknown. The doctor can tell me his doctor's lingua; but ultimately whose report will I believe? I will choose to believe in the report of The Lord. The act of believing means to trust and rely on faith. Believing means accepting the contents of a matter because it is what you trust to be true. So, this week my child, I am accepting the truth that God will perfect all that concerns you and me. I accept that He will never neglect us—*we are etched in the palm of His hands*. I am choosing to believe that our Heavenly Father is True and Faithful and that settles all my anxiety. In fact, I have CHOSEN to believe the divine manuscripts which show that our God is intimately involved with His children. I will not allow anything or anyone to shake my belief in Him. He has proven to be *more than enough*!

Dear Children,

Despite the changes all around, there is one thing that remains constant and that is God's love for you. The noise around you tries to suggest to you a roadmap of what this journey will entail. Just a heads up, **God is not accepting suggestions for the next steps that you will take**. Your life is already mapped out and all that you will go through will work together for good. Your life is a divine orchestration. Each piece of your life will play its musical note under the directive of the master of the orchestra. Some of the musical pieces may seem out of tune but wait......Listen carefully! The accompanying notes will bring harmony and completion to your unanswered questions. Your Heavenly Father is not trying to figure things out as you move from one stage to another. He is the director of your life's orchestra, and every note is in sync. The disruptions are permitted by The Divine One. Please realize that even though He has permitted some things to happen in your life, it does not mean that He approved of all of your decisions. Notwithstanding, He has given permission and divine ordination and will include it into your life's orchestra as an accent point. *"For my thoughts are not your thoughts, neither are your ways my ways, saith the Lord. For as the heavens are higher than the earth, so are my ways higher than your ways, and my thoughts than your thoughts"* (Isaiah 55: 8-9, KJV). The Master Designer is signaling to you that He is aware of ALL of you. This journey is a display of what He can do in you and through you. He has retained the I Am that I Am position—**He cannot change**.

WEEK 14

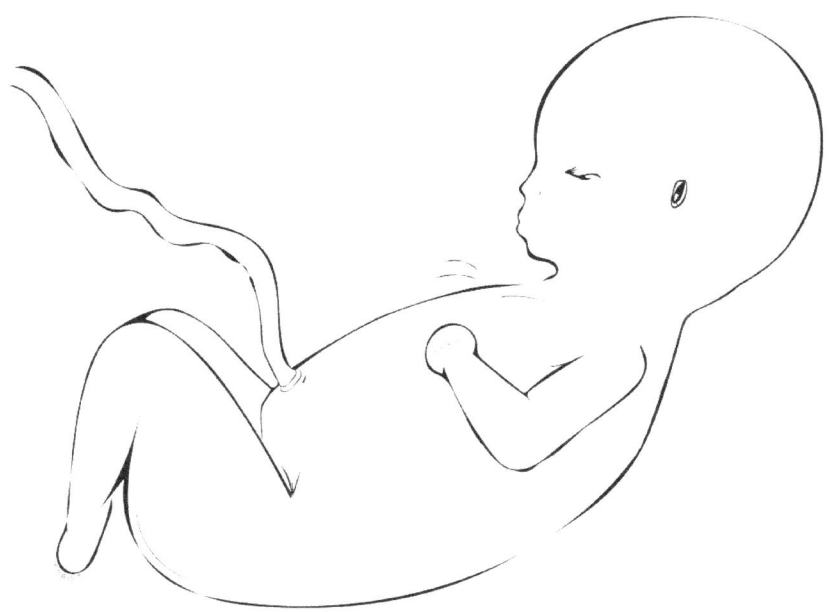

I am about the size of a peach.

3.42in/8.7cm long

But now, O Lord, thou art our father; we are the clay, and thou our potter; and we all are the work of thy hand.

Isaiah 64: 8

Dear Mom,

It is Week 14, and you should be adjusting to being pregnant. I heard the nausea, and tiredness is not as profound at this stage of the journey. If you are not feeling better Mom, please remember, I am depending on you, and remember that we can do this together. We are a team! This week Mom, I may be getting some hair on my head. Instead of my head leaning on my chest, I am actually going to have a *neck!* My heartbeat will be beating approximately twice as much as yours. This week I can frown, I can squint, and some people think that I may be able to smile. Smile-camera-action!!!!!!! I am getting ready for my photoshoot. And I am certainly getting ready to see you. Oh, how much I love you, Mom.

Dear Child,

This week marks the beginning of our second trimester together. We are both still here to finish authoring our story. Your heartbeat reminds me that your life is precious. I rejoice in the God of my salvation because you are wonderfully made.

"What is man, that thou art mindful of him? and the son of man, that thou visitest him? For thou hast made him a little lower than the angels, and hast crowned him with glory and honour" (Psalm 6:4-5, KJV). Oh my child, my God is concerned about you? He has come to give you life—*precious life*. In this trimester He is just as concerned about you and me as He was at the start of the journey. He is not just involved in the forming of you. He **IS** forming you. He is not merely involved because it is His good pleasure to fashion you. **You are His!**

Dear Children,

The **I AM,** is with you and He is for you. The stress of this journey can be compounded if you rely on yourself. When God decided to bring you into existence, He had no reason to reveal His plans. Therefore, trying to understand God is going to leave you frustrated and overwhelmed. Your best option is to trust Him. Running ahead of God is the formula to viewing a life's event as the end of the world. The urge of wanting a full scoop of your future equates to a life that is spiritually out of balance. This journey is marked by stages, and each stage is placed in the correct order by the master designer. Use this journey to practice your faith-muscle. This practice will keep you connected to your Heavenly Father. The entirety of this journey will be a fulfillment of a complete life that is yielded to a God that can be trusted. There are moments when you will feel a strong urge to be fearful, and that is the cue to put on your faith-breathing mask and call on the name of The Lord. When you are afraid and your SELF is overwhelmed by your prolonged thoughts of the future, restore your strength in His words. *"What time I am afraid, I will trust in thee. In God I will praise his word, In God I have put my trust;......."* (Psalm 56:3-4a, KJV). One of the byproducts of relying on self is the inevitable realization of fear. The resulting outcome of fear occurs because there is a point when everyone recognizes that self is insufficient in the presence of life's demands. Save yourself the heartache and headache—trust the one who is True and Faithful.

WEEK 15

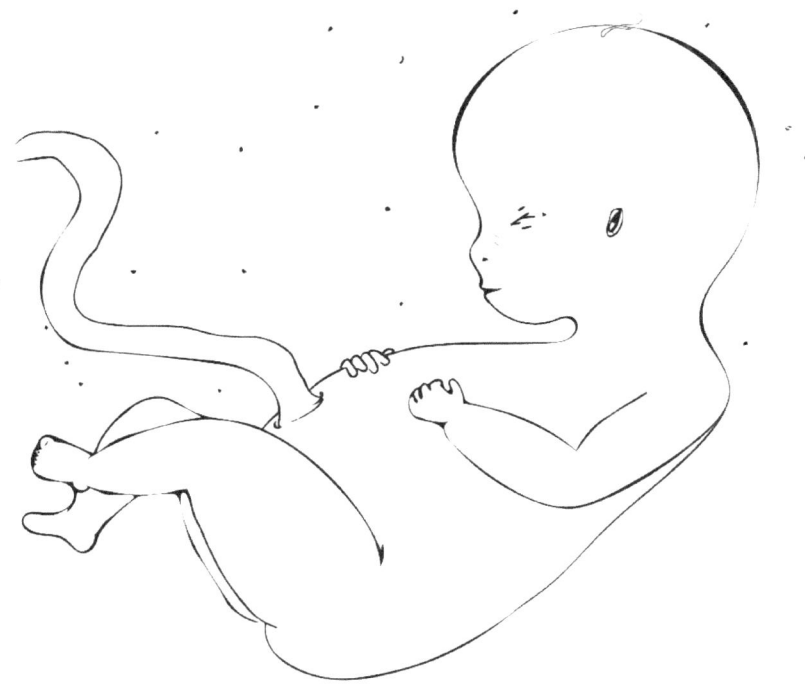

I am about the size of an apple.

3.98in/10.1cm long

But thou art he that took me out of the womb: thou didst make me hope when I was upon my mother's breasts.

Psalm 22: 9

Dear Mom,

This week I am weighing a little less than 3.5-ounces. I am still very small, but I am moving around a lot. The times and the days when I am not sleeping, you should start feeling me move. I am breathing and I am also sucking and swallowing. I have arms and legs, and I am just moving them. I am not fully coordinated and I do not think I want to be. All I want to do is move and move and move and then sleep and sleep and sleep and sleep and sleep. This week, small bones in my inner ear are forming. Mom, guess what my sweet mom? I will be able to hear your voice, so you can start singing to me. You can say hi to me. I am beginning to feel our emotional connection, Mom. You and me…….. I am getting bigger and longer. I am growing for sure! Start singing Mom and I will start dancing for you. I like to move it, I like to move it, move it, move it!!!!

Dear Child,

You are 3 and one-half ounces big (laugh out loud)! I cannot imagine 3 and one-half pounds being big; but, in the fetus world you are B-I-G. I am still standing in amazement of how everything came into being. From a cell…….. and look at what you are today. Oh, I now know how great the responsibility is to imprint marks of wisdom, love, and grace on you. I am in total wonderment that I have been selected by heaven to be the hands and the feet that will hold you and walk you through some dark spaces that life may bring. I know I cannot do it alone, and I do not want to do it alone. So, I will trust the Divine One, The God of Israel, Jehovah, The Mighty Warrior, and our Redeemer. He will carry us both, and I will listen to His instructions on how to guide you and show you the path that you should take in life. I cannot do this alone and so I will trust Him. Each day I am using it to prepare myself on how to be a mother -your mom.

Dear Children,

Approach this week with a willingness to surrender your *Me-centric* behaviors. Do not be surprised that your *Me-agenda* does not match with God's agenda. Isaiah 55: 8, KJV echoes *"For my thoughts are not your thoughts, neither are your ways my ways, saith the LORD."* Your Heavenly Father's agenda is in sync with heavenly things while your agenda is situated in earthly realms. You cannot expect God's will to be fulfilled in your life while trying to jostle for your willingness to submit your agenda. He is such a patient father so He will not fight you to sit on the throne of your heart. A will can only be executed upon the submitting of someone's rights. Your right to have an opinion about your life is actually a privilege called *choice*. Do not be fooled by the freedom of an opinion. Ultimately, your Heavenly Father's plans for your life are far better than your self-controlling ideas. *"A man's heart deviseth his way: But the LORD directeth his steps"* (Proverbs 16:9, KJV). Strive to relinquish your desire to be the other driver who is seated in the passenger's seat. Your Father does not need a copilot! Do not use your backseat GPS ideas to demand Him to follow your directions. Take your hand off the steering wheel.......**This journey is fully planned, and all the critical pieces are out of your control but not out of control.** Give up the fantasy idea that a life that is controlled by God has no challenges. In reality a life that is fully dependent on God displays a peace that cannot be explained by human's attempts. This journey marks a new chapter in your life which is entitled *Trust God*!

WEEK 16

I am about the size of a small avocado.

4.57in/11.6cm long

I was cast upon thee from the womb: thou art my God from my mother's belly.

Psalm 22: 10

Dear Mom,

This week you will be going to multiple doctor visits. You will have to do tests for anemia, infections, diseases, blood type, and many more pokes with needles. They hurt……. put all jokes aside, those needles hurt. But because you love me, you are willing to do it for me. Thanks Mom. By the way, I can also move my eyes sideways, even though my eyelids are still sealed for protection. The muscles in my eyes are starting to work. When bright light shines on your womb, I can actually sense the brightness of the lights. When the lights are too bright for my eyes, I simply cuddle myself up and close my eyes tighter. Also, my dearest mom, please be careful how you talk about me and what you say about me, because I can now hear you mom. Did you just say you love me? *I love you more Mom.* This week I found my umbilical cord, and I am holding on to it. Calm down Mom, do not worry! My grip is not strong enough, so I cannot hurt you or stop the flow of blood. I am just practicing using my little fingers and toes. I am just checking out my body parts. By the way, you can start playing music for me too, and you can start praying over me. I love all different genres of music, especially your original songs. Your songs are better, Mom. You have talent.

Dear Child,

Every day is not great at this stage of our journey. However, I am learning to appreciate every milestone that I have with you and to carry you. The doctors' visits are not always exciting because I am pricked and poked and I have to make changes to who I used to be. Now I am mom and everything I do is to make sure you are in good health. Oh, dear child, your Heavenly Father beauty exudes, and his attention to details boggles my mind. His glory lives inside of me as He lives through you. *"Know ye that the Lord he is God: it is he that hath made us, and not we ourselves; we are his people, and the sheep of his pasture"* (Psalm 100: 3, KJV). We are HIS- ***you are His and I am His***. He is that good Shepherd and he bids us to walk beside Him. Oh, my dear child you are His and the beauty of the living God is upon you. Oh, open your eyes and see that the Lord is good. *"It is he that has made us and not we of ourselves"* (Psalm 100: 3b, KJV). Let us walk this journey, knowing that He is good and He is that Good Shepherd. We belong to him. Oh, my dear child, The Lord is good!

Dear Children,

There is nothing in this life that you will ever face alone- absolutely NOTHING. If there is an area in your life where you feel as if God has left you alone, it is because you have left Him out of the equation. Your fixation on your *tomorrows* is hindering your appreciation of your *todays*. This journey is layered with patience. Begin to see patience as a form of nutrient that you must consume every day. Even your doctors cannot predict God's next move. Satan always tries to undermine what God has accomplished in your life, and you oftentimes allow this defeated foe to interject himself into your life. You have listened to him through the noise all around you. God is softly nudging you back into His divine presence where you can center yourself on things that are eternal. *"For our light affliction, which is but for a moment, worketh for us a far more exceeding and eternal weight of glory; while we look not at the things which are seen, but at the things which are not seen: for the things which are seen are temporal; but the things which are not seen are eternal."* (2 Corinthians 4:17-18, KJV). The yearning in your soul results only in negative energy. Whenever you feel crushed by the weight of your tomorrows, remind yourself that God is present in your todays and your tomorrows. Release your worries into the hands of God and resist the desire to be anxious. Your anxiety is a result of your willingness to believe what others have spoken over your life. Convert negative suggestions that are sent your way into words of hope. Use your intimate time of spending time in God's presence as a weapon to erase doubts and fears. This journey is a reminder that God is above ALL things—*even your heartaches and headaches*. Whenever you feel as if you are drowning in your tomorrows, verbalize your trust in your Heavenly Father. *"And Peter answered him and said, Lord, if it be thou, bid me come unto thee on the water. And he said, Come. And when Peter was come down out of the ship, he walked on the water, to go to Jesus. But when he saw the wind boisterous, he was afraid; and beginning to sink, he cried, saying, Lord, save me"* (Matthew 14:28-30, KJV). What are you focusing on? The challenges of the journey or on Jesus? If fear is allowed to gain territory in your heart, you will begin to sink. Turn your eyes on Jesus and the wind of your life will cease to disrupt your journey. The wind will blow, but because you are in the presence of the Master, the wind have no power to take you off course.

WEEK 17

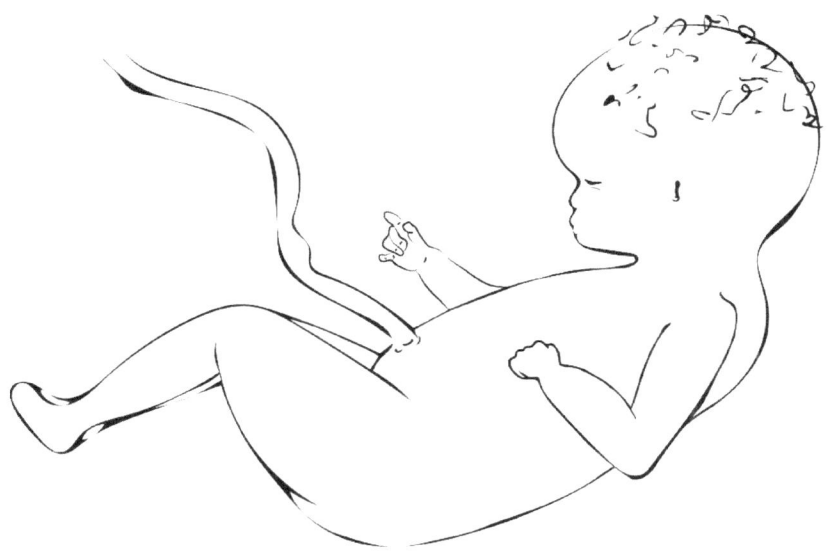

I am about the size of a pear.

5.12in/13cm long

Thine hands have made me and fashioned me together round about (8a);

Job 10:8a

Dear Mom,

Mom, I am growing so quickly and within the last 2 weeks my weight has doubled. From head to my bottom, I am 5 inches long. My translucent skin is like a window in to my body. You can see the blood vessels which are supplying oxygenated blood to my entire body. Calcium is now being deposited in my tiny bones. If I am a girl, my ovaries are cramped with 3 million eggs- *that will be all the eggs that I will have in my lifetime!* My identity is being formed, and I am learning how to stretch and exercise my muscles. This week, I am getting all my fingerprints and now I know how unique I have been created. Imagine that no two individuals that The Master Designer has created have the same prints. Mom, I am me! What a miracle my dearest Mom.

Dear Child,

I stand in amazement of His glory. Each day, I sense His presence as you live inside of me. I sense this nearness of a God who humbled himself and came to earth and lived among men. It is the same God who has placed you inside of me. He is so interested in every detail of your well-being. It is the same God who parted the Red Sea. He is the same yesterday, today and forevermore. He cannot change and He will not change. He is who He said He is. It is the same God who cared for His son as He lived inside of the Virgin Mary. Then we, my dear child can rest………Shhhhh……. BE STILL. He has given the assurance that it is His presence and His love that will carry you inside of me. I am confident that He will care for you the very same way He loved His dear son Jesus Christ, as He was carried in His mother's womb. His character embodies love because He is love. Then you and I, my child, are in the hands of a God who is a loving Father.

Dear Children,

God's divine orchestration of your existence is like none other in the universe. His love is layered in every facet of your life. On the days when you feel a sense of hopelessness, revisit your purpose and reaffirm your trust in God. As you spend more time in His presence, your need for God will become more pronounced and you will become more aware of the frailty of your nature. As the clay in His hands, the longer you take to relinquish your compulsive nature to dictate your roadmap, the more difficult it will be to trust God's guidance. Being preoccupied with your roadmap places you above God. A life that prioritizes *self* over God's plans resembles idolatry. This journey requires less of self. The intricacies of each stage of this journey are extremely critical. So, the less of *self* that shows up will give you complete access to your Heavenly Father and His lordship. God will never give you such a crucial assignment and abandon you to figure it out without His help. *"But mine eyes are unto thee, O GOD the Lord: In thee is my trust; ...."* (Psalm 141:8a, KJV). You are a participant in this holy moment. Notwithstanding, you are not a consultant for the layout of the tapestry of the plans. God has invited you into a relationship that uses a currency of trust. The lack of trust suggests that you doubt His credibility, which signals that you are not confident that He is qualified for this life-event. Bring this human nature under the lordship of the Heavenly Father as a witness to the evil one that you are not a fan of a lie that he once tried to use to disrupt heaven. It is satan's wish that mankind would doubt the character of God. You are accustomed to listening to satan's lies and to resist this behavior will require you to drown out his voice with the truth found in God's holy words. Change your perspective of whose you are and begin to realign the purpose you were created for in this life. Realigning your mindset will allow you to gain clarity in reference to the infusion of God's sovereignty in this journey. When you encounter a problem on this journey, raise your awareness of God's presence and you will begin to see how He views you. *".........; but though our outward man perish, yet the inward man is renewed day by day"* (2 Corinthians 4:16, KJV). Rest in God's divine sovereignty. In Him you have life and life more abundantly.

WEEK 18

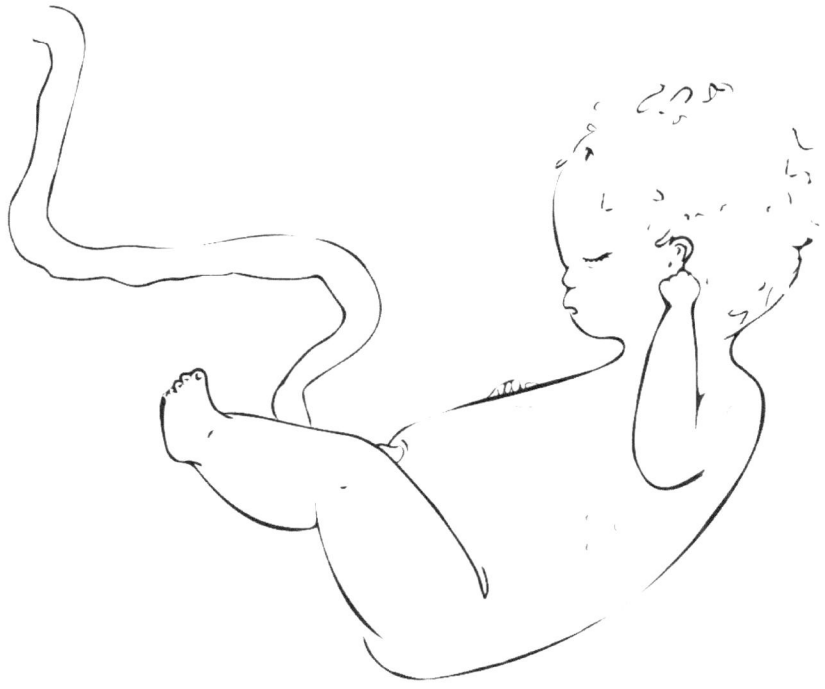

I am about the size of a bell pepper.

5.59in/14.2cm long

Thou hast granted me life and favor, and thy visitation hath preserved my spirit.

Job 10:12

Dear Mom,

This is an exciting week for you and me. You are now able to feel every twitch and move that I make inside of you. You will feel flutters. Every time I knock on your uterus, it feels like I am knocking on your door. It feels like a tickle or maybe a whisper. You are becoming more conscious of my every move. You can feel me when you are laying down or sitting still. You are becoming more aware of me, and I am becoming more aware of you. We are developing our own *love-language*. It is just you and me, Mom. By the way, it is getting a little tight living inside of you. Space is now limited because now you have to house me, the amniotic fluid, the membranes, the umbilical cord, and the placenta. All of these critical pieces must fit inside of you. No wonder you are feeling so tired and feel as if you are going to burst. I owe you big time, *Thanks for carrying me, Mom.*

Dear Child,

"I am the resurrection, and the life: he that believeth in me, though he were dead, yet shall he live: And whosoever liveth and believeth in me shall never die. Believest thou this?" (John 11: 25 and 26, KJV). Oh, my child, God is life and He gives life. Our God is a resurrector of dead things. He controls both the living and the dead. He has the capacity to bring things back to life. Then why should you and I worry? Why should we even fear? There is no power on earth that controls both life and death. But our God, my dear child, controls them both. This journey that gives you life, is totally controlled by Him. He is indeed in control of the universe, my dear child. We are a part of the universe and so He sees you and He sees me. Before He formed you, He knew you!

Dear Children,

The path that you are on is a part of a divine plan. While society gives you the idea that you control your destiny, the reality is you cannot control what you do not own. Your life is not a lottery game that is dictated by how well you play the numbers. This belief of control is not supported by the divine manuscript- God's holy bible. *"And which of you with taking thought can add to his stature one cubit? If ye then be not able to do that thing which is least, why take ye thought for the rest?"* (Luke 12:25-26, KJV). The creator of all things has vested interest in your wellbeing, and

He will not sit idly and watch you **self-diagnose** and **self-design** a life that is not yours. Relax in the awareness that the master designer who created and controls your life can be trusted. There is nothing that you need, He cannot provide. The timing of when and what you think you need are oftentimes what causes you to become anxious. This tendency is anchored in fear and self-reliance. There is no security in your makeshift self-indulging plans. If you choose to be honest, you will realize that your life is being sabotaged by your tendency to compare your life with others. When you take your eyes off your Heavenly Father you will continue to jostle for a type of self-worth that is defined by society. If you make it your duty to let God define your worth, He will place a value on you based on your purpose. You were created by Him, and it is only Him that has the final word on the path your life should explore. Focus on your Heavenly Father! *"Thou wilt keep him in perfect peace, whose mind is stayed on thee: because he trusteth in thee. Trust ye in the LORD for ever: for in the LORD JEHOVAH is everlasting strength:"* (Isaiah 26:3-4, KJV). Remember that He goes before you and clears the path. Nothing you are experiencing or will ever go through can take Him by surprise. Whenever you feel frustrated, ***release the reins and give God full authority to handle the situation***. Do not push against every bump in the road. These hiccups are designed as opportunities to fully rely on your Heavenly Father. These moments possess elements that can undress *SELF*. Learn to cultivate seeds of faith in a God who intimately knows you-*"Know ye that the LORD he is God: It is he that hath made us, and not we ourselves;...,."* (Psalm 100:3, KJV). Trust your Heavenly Father and let Him guide you through this journey. He will accomplish great things in your life in accordance with His timing. Society's views of who controls destiny is seated in ideologies that are far removed from Biblical teachings and are rooted in satanic teachings. Do not anchor your life on these disillusionments—*they are not God-sanctioned!* This journey is a masterpiece of His power, and you have been chosen to be a part of this divine transaction between heaven and earth.

WEEK 19

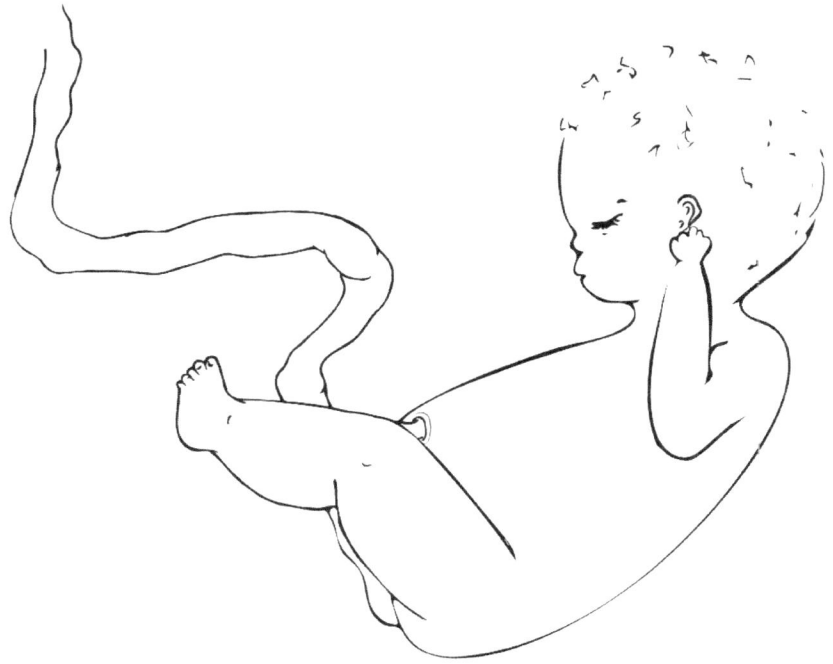

I am about the size of a mango.

6.02 inches/15.3 cm long

As thou knowest not what is the way of the spirit, nor how the bones do grow in the womb of her that is with child: even so thou knowest not the works of God who maketh all.

Ecclesiastes 11:5

Dear Mom,

Yippee!!!!! We are almost midpoint through this pregnancy journey. Big changes are occurring in your body and in my body. I am no longer that tiny thing that started out with you. I am getting bigger and stronger, and the plan for my life is getting clear. I am more than 5 and one-half inches long and my skin is so translucent that every vein can be seen through my skin. There is this white greasy substance that is covering my skin. It looks yucky! But I need it to keep my vital organs protected from extreme temperatures. My kidneys are working really well this week, and they are producing urine which is a large percentage of amniotic fluid. By the way, if you want to find out my gender; this week is a perfect week to see if I am a boy or a girl. And this week is even better to see the development of my spine, my heart, and all my vital organs. I am developed and I am fully human. Mom, I am created by a power that is greater than you and me. You need to get to know the greater power that is at work in me and you. I believe both you and I are in a divine plan. Let's get to know whose we are and who is really in control and at work on this journey.

Dear Child,

For I know whom I have believed, and I am persuaded that this journey has been orchestrated by a God that is greater than any human force. I am even more convinced that He is able to keep that which is in His care until the full completion is realized. I believe that our God is able, my dear child. He formed you when there was none of you. This week, you embody His power, His glory, His Majesty and His infinite love. I cannot begin to tell you how much having you on the inside of me has brought me closer to His presence. I am not sure what each day will bring, but I am sure who governs my past, present and future. My dear child, fear and faith cannot coexist. So today I choose to have the spirit of faith dwelling inside my innermost being. I cannot wait for the day when I get to tell you more about Him. I do not know all about him, but together we can get to learn who He is, and why He has chosen to love and care for us.

Dear Children,

One of the nuggets of this journey is learning how to be still. There is much to be learned from the beauty of remaining still. The hush of the noise around you is one thing that you should begin craving. Silence holds the capacity to breathe a fresh breath of life into your being. For it is in silence you begin to create, and it is in silence you can become great. This mysterious stillness, when it seems as if nothing is happening, is actually when a 'behind-the-scenes' movement is underway. *"Be still, and know that I am God: ...."* (Psalm 46:10a, KJV) continues to ring true the connection of God's presence being infused in the stillness of our lives. *"And they heard the voice of the LORD God walking in the garden in the cool of the day: ...."* (Genesis 3:8a, KJV). To hear God's voice requires you to seek out ways to host His presence. Find a space in your world where you can be **present** in His *presence*. Create a time when you can mute your noise and prioritize entertaining your Heavenly Father's presence. This may be challenging, as there are many things that are fighting to get your attention. However, overtime you will begin to discover that an empty cistern cannot fill a cup. Neither can a withdrawal be made from an empty bank account. You must allot time in your schedule—*quality time to be deposited in by your Heavenly Father.* You must use this journey to become a receptacle of His presence. As you continue on this journey you will become more aware of the sources of your burnouts and frustrations- the triggers that drain you and leave you feeling hopeless. These are the areas that you need to step away from and zone into that quiet place. As you begin polishing this skill of *stepping away*, you will discover that stepping away sometimes means entering a virtual space of peace. That means, you can still be in the crowd and the noise, but you have mentally vacated the space. This practice of *stepping away* will begin to restore your spirit and cause you to find balance in your life. This practice has therapeutic benefits and now you can become more available to be a reservoir of life to others. **There is healing in Hisnce presence.!!**

WEEK 20

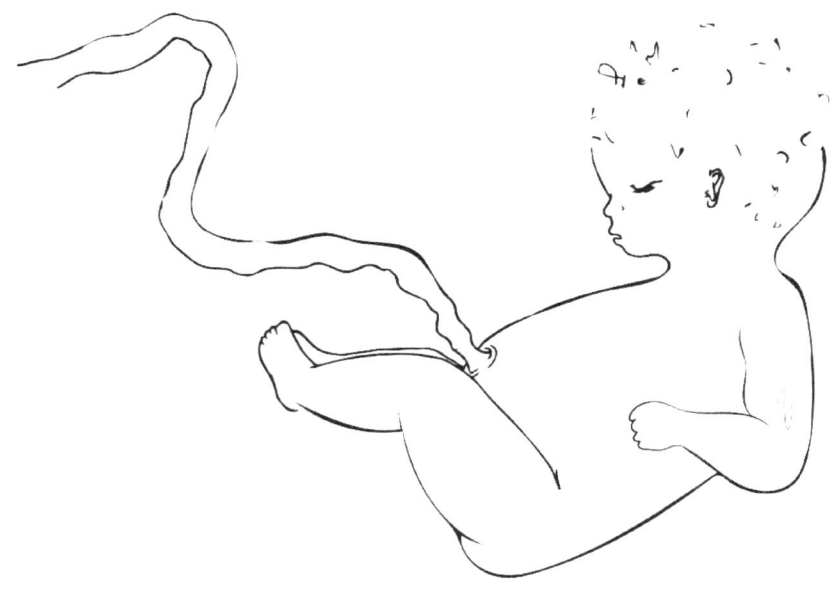

I am about the size of a banana.

6.46in/16.4cm long

Every good gift and every perfect gift is from above, and cometh down from the Father of lights, with whom is no variableness, neither shadow of turning.

James 1: 17

Dear Mom,

Hey mom, we are officially halfway through the pregnancy journey. The doctor may give you a due date for when I will arrive, but do not get too fixated on that date. I can arrive two weeks before or after the 40th (fortieth) week., or I may arrive even earlier. Right now, I do not know because I am not in control of when I will arrive. Remember that I told you that you and I are just a part of the divine plan. Having said that……. *We are not in charge of when I will arrive.* By the way, I can hear every sound that is made outside of you (for the most part). I know that you are curious about my growth, so, this week I am about 6 and one-half inches long from the top of my head to my bottom. My skin is fully covered in the greasy white stuff that I told you about and I am swimming and moving about in approximately 10 ounces of amniotic fluid. At this stage, you should have become more increasingly aware of my every move. Every day, I take longer naps but when I am awake, I am up and moving. I know you are getting tired and you are getting bigger, but soon we will meet face-to-face, and it all will be over.

Dear Child,

Even when I cannot see His hands, I know that He is working inside of me. I also know that our Heavenly Father is interested in changing our lives. He has changed mine because of you. Having you inside of me has increased my dependence on Him. There is less of me and more of Him. Since your arrival, I cannot imagine living my life outside of Him. It took this journey with you for me to get closer to Him, so my dear child I am so thankful for you. Each day I awake, and I feel the prodding of you inside of me-*I sense life*……. We are indeed in his hands. My dear child, grew up to be a man or a woman that serves Him- *a person who places full trust in Him.* Each day that draws closer to the day when you enter my world, reminds me of the honor that has been given to me to teach you the path of righteousness, and to reflect His glory to you. You are truly a blessing in my life. Love you, my dear little one.

Dear Children,

Use each day to polish your peace. This journey can frazzle your peace especially if you begin wandering from the peace giver. The intense desire to wonder how you will cope with the surmounting changes is enough to make you blow a fuse. Instead of becoming fixated with the ups and downs of this journey begin to mentally rehearse your Heavenly Father's promises. *"The LORD shall command the blessing upon thee......Blessed shall be the fruit of thy body......,And the LORD shall make thee plenteous in goods, in the fruit of thy body, And all these blessings shall come on thee, and overtake thee,............"* (Deuteronomy 28: 4a, 8a, 11a, and 2a, KJV). Challenging times often distract you from seeing your blessings. However, challenging times should serve as cues that you are eligible for divine intervention. Your blessings are reserved; therefore, problems cannot erase which have been promised to you. Reframe your problems. See them as opportunities for God to unveil His power to you. During these challenging times, remember, your Heavenly Father does not have to prove himself to you. It is you who waver in your thoughts towards Him. Rest assured that His thoughts towards you are good and not evil. Utilize this journey as a way to adjust your lenses—*you need to begin to see your Heavenly Father for who He is and not for what you think He should be.* Trust that He knows what He is doing, and He is in control of your circumstances. Be secure in His promises.

WEEK 21

I am about the size of a carrot.

10.51in/26.7cm long

Blessed shall be the fruit of thy body, and the fruit of thy ground, and the fruit of thy cattle, the increase of thy kine, and the flocks of thy sheep.

Deuteronomy 28: 4

Dear Mom,

I know that it is becoming difficult for you to sleep, and I am very sorry Mom. Look on the bright side of things—you are getting used to me waking up in the middle of the night. After all, it is not too terrible, because you can sing to me bedtime lullabies. This week, I am the size of a carrot, and I weigh about 12 ounces. I am still tiny, but I am growing according to the divine plan. My brain and muscles are working in sync, so I am not just bouncing around without a purpose. I am not sure how, but the amniotic fluid is kind of tasty. I am using the fluid to practice my swallowing and digesting skills. There is also some waste matter that is being prepared in my bowels. Not to worry, I will be passing it out when I make my grand entrance in your world. By the way, my tooth buds are getting up to speed, and I will be a little more prepared for my photoshoot (laugh out loud).

Dear Child,

What a mighty God we serve! The angels bow and worship him. There is so much to worship him for—*and that the angels know*. Therefore, worshiping Him continuously, it is their joy, it is their delight because He deserves our worship. This week I do not want to just praise him. I want to worship him. Praise simply means that I am happy for what He has given me. But worship says to Him, no matter what happens in this journey, you are worthy of all the worship and the adoration. This week I resound in my heart that, the Lord giveth and the Lord taketh, blessed be His name. He has given you to me, my dear child, and so I bless his name. His decisions are not only final—**they are good for me**. His thoughts towards me are thoughts of life, joy and peace. So, we can rest in his presence.

Dear Children,

Begin to see this journey as a Sabbath—a time that is dedicated for rest and worship. The busyness around you can drain your spiritual energy and leave you feeling fatigued. This overwhelming surge of activities has the power to throw you off your axis and destabilize your focus. While this journey is typically filled with the surrounding noise, you must intentionally remove yourself from the environment. Disconnect the cables of your *must-do agenda* and purposefully attach yourself to a heavenly place. Remember this journey is a critical moment where heaven makes a transaction with earth. You have been entrusted with the care of a living soul. You have the God-given opportunity to place your imprints on another life. Devote yourself to spending time in your Heavenly Father's presence and deposit in others only what has been deposited in you. Find comfort in knowing that you do not have to bear this burden alone. You have been equipped for this journey, and your God will never entrust anything to you unless He knows that He has prepared you. He gives grace to those who ask. He will lavish you with His favor- simply ask…….. *"If any of you lack wisdom, let him ask of God, that giveth to all men liberally, ……..; and it shall be given him. But let him ask in faith, nothing wavering………"* (James 1:5-6a, KJV). This journey is indeed an opportunity for you to step away from the jostle and find a quiet place to seek that which has eternal meaning.

WEEK 22

I am about the size of a papaya.

10.94in/27.8cm long

*But now thus saith the Lord
that created thee, O Jacob, and
he that formed thee, O Israel,
Fear not: for I have redeemed
thee, I have called thee by thy
name; thou art mine.*

Isaiah 43:1

Dear Mom,

My eyelids are still closed tightly but I am getting better at detecting when you have turned on the lights. I am super excited because I will soon start opening my eyes…...I cannot wait! I have been sucking my thumb Mom—I have been naughty. This week, I have spent most of my time hiccupping, grabbing my umbilical cord, and strengthening my grasp. Your womb is like a trampoline. By the way, my skin is not as translucent and so my blood vessels and veins are not very obvious to the naked eye. Mom, my weeks here inside your body have been absolutely wonderful. I am living inside of you and each day I realize that this journey has been ordained. It is not by chance that I am here. Thanks for placing value on the sacredness of *my life*. I know the culture tells you that you have the right to do whatever you want with your body, so Mom, I am forever grateful that you have embraced me. Thanks so much for partnering with heaven to honor my life. **I love you, Mom!**

Dear Child,

As you grow inside of me, I am growing in Him. I can feel His glory around you. I feel the angels have come to dwell with me and to guide my steps. The angels know that you belong to the Most High God. They have been created just a little lower than the angels. It is their duty and pleasure to watch over us. You have angels assigned to you, my dear child. Angels are already working to protect you. As you grow inside of me, sense their presence. *"The angel of the Lord encampeth round about them that fear him, and delivereth them"* (Psalm 34: 7, KJV). Angels are surrounding us, my dear child because we have placed our full trust in our Heavenly Father.

Dear Children,

As you continue on this journey you will notice that there are some rough terrains that you are required to travel. Every day is not peachy, and your Heavenly Father knows! If you begin to count up the bad days and the good days, you will discover that the good days outweigh the bad days. There are not necessarily more good days but what it is, as you begin to tally the circumstances in order to categorize whether or not a day is good or bad, you will discover that God has been present in every single circumstance. His presence makes the difference in you making a decision about each day. Your Heavenly Father is a God of **presence** rather than **presents**. *"Fear thou not; FOR I AM WITH THEE: be not dismayed; for I am thy God: I will strengthen thee; yea, I will help thee; yea, I will uphold thee with the right hand of my righteousness"* (Isaiah 41:10, KJV). If you waver in your confidence, retreat to God's presence and re-establish your trust in your God. *"For I am the LORD, I change not......"* (Malachi 3: 6a, KJV). The constant is GOD. Although this journey is filled with turbulence, your Heavenly Father remains the same yesterday, today, and forever. You can rest your confidence on this immutable truth. Your God never changes. This knowledge or awakening should infuse your soul with peace. Such realization will catapult you into becoming appreciative of the good and bad days. You are appreciative because you now understand that you are not alone. This means that what once bothered you is now viewed as a stepping-stone into greatness. Good days and bad days, I cannot complain!

WEEK 23

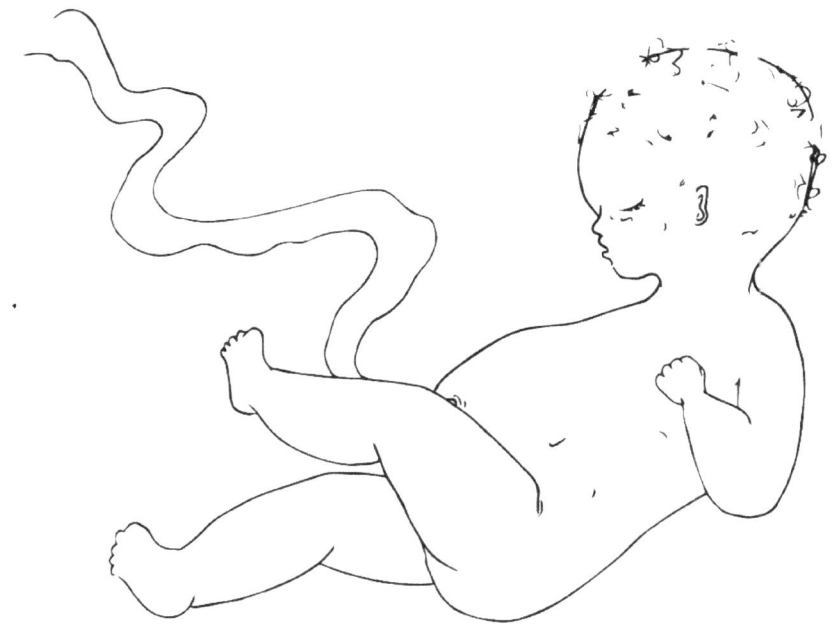

I am about the size of a grapefruit.

11.38in/28.9cm long

Thus saith the Lord, thy redeemer,and he that formed thee from the womb, I am the Lord that maketh all things; that stretcheth forth the heavens alone; that spreadeth abroad the earth by myself;

Isaiah 44: 24

Dear Mom,

Have I been showing up in your dreams? This week is the start of many vivid dreams, and I was wondering if you have seen me in a starring role. Laugh out loud. I am dying with laughter, even though I know that they are your subconscious working overtime. At this stage of my journey, I am weighing about one pound and from the top of my head to my little bottom, I am 8 inches long. My lungs are getting ready to exhale as this week they are forming a substance that will keep my alveoli open at birth. Just for giggles, my ears are fully functioning, so each time a dog barks or whenever you slam the door, I can react. Let's just say, I am jittery when there is a sudden loud noise. No pressure my dearest Mom, I love the sound of your voice.

Dear Child,

Each day that draws us closer to the day of your delivery marks another milestone of blessings. Let us count a few of the blessings.

(1) You and I are alive.

(2) I have the courage to carry and embrace you as mine.

(3) Your organs are being formed.

(4) You are loved.

(5) We are more than halfway through our journey.

These blessings are worth celebrating. I am learning daily that when I focus on my blessings, the challenges of life seem almost nonexistent. Trust me, my child, I know that the struggles are still here, but I am learning to change my perspective. Being pregnant is not always 'cookies and cream.' The more I talk to you, I am motivated to buy a calculator to add up all my blessings. I am ecstatic that I have the favor of God upon my life. Of course, my dear child, life will give you lemons. But I have found a way to use those lemons to make a lemon pie or a cup of lemonade. Because of you, my little one, my perspective is changing. You being here, reminds me that my challenges are a part of a divine orchestration. There is a mastermind behind all of this called LIFE. My challenges are blessings in disguise.

Dear Children,

Happiness is not found in having the things you want; rather, happiness is appreciating the things that have been given to you. This may not be a *red-carpet* experience but if correctly viewed, this experience is a training exercise for the cultivation of patience, humility, self-denial, and trust. The main thing that is at work is not a new life entering this world; but it is a place where your Heavenly Father can get your attention to change YOU. This masterpiece that is underway includes making room for The Holy presence of God to dwell inside you. Making room will require a *deep cleaning* of behaviors and habits that you have been holding on to prior to the start of this journey. Some of these cherished practices have become a part of who you are as a person, and you know that it is time to change. I am also using this journey to trim away some of the people in your life that are not depositing currency in your *heaven-bank*; instead, they are making withdrawals from your *soul's depository* which have left you spiritually bankrupt. I know that you believe that you cannot imagine living without them but these 'soulmates' are depleting your **God-connection**. Yield your will to your Heavenly Father and allow him to remove the people and practices that are clogging the path that the Holy Spirit needs to flow through you. This is a painful process, but God knows what is best for you. Use this journey as a point in your life that you surrender your **ME-living**. If you were honest and stop resisting The Holy Spirit's voice, you would realize that you have issued too many 'keys' to your life and people are still able to access you even though they are no longer a part of your life. Allow The Holy Spirit to change the entrance point of your life so that these 'old keys' will not be able to access you and trigger your abandoned practices. The narrative that this journey is governed by the intense cravings of an unborn *who is yet to develop a set of preferences* is not in alignment with truth. These cravings are stemming from deep-rooted desires, and in this journey, they are surfacing as uncontrollable behaviors and desires to surrender your will to please SELF. Cravings (Old English-crafians) are selfish demands that are dictating your behaviors. This word (cravings) conveys the idea that the source of the demands has rights to make the claims. You are not governed by a force that has a right to make demands upon your desires and behaviors. There is a root cause for this unrestrained or unruly desire. Bring these intense desires to the foot of the cross and allow The Holy Spirit to destroy or address the root cause of the unrelenting stimulation. Do not use this journey as an excuse to

92

over-indulge or engage in behaviors that fuel the demands of the flesh. *"Submit yourselves therefore to God. Resist the devil, and he will flee from you. Draw nigh to God, and he will draw nigh to you………."* (James 4:7-8a, KJV). Submission requires conviction and it is the act of relinquishing to another party to decide over a matter. What results from the submission is within your jurisdiction to decide. Relinquish your rights of your desires and behaviors and allow The Holy Spirit to govern your decisions. This experience is intended to realign you for the next chapter of your life's journey. Release your strongholds and let Him who created you have full access. *"And he said unto me, My grace is sufficient for thee: for my strength is made perfect in weakness. Most gladly therefore will I rather glory in my infirmities, that the power of Christ may rest upon me. Therefore I take pleasure in infirmities, in reproaches, in necessities, in persecutions, in distresses for Christ's sake: for when I am weak, then am I strong"* *(2 Corinthians 12: 9-10, KJV)*. **If and when you are able to master self-control during this journey, you are strategically positioning yourself to be aligned with your purpose and divine calling.**

SUBMISSION

O Lord may my womb be a sanctuary of praise
And not a tomb for my borrowed days
An altar of sacrifice
And not a house for the evil one lies
O Lord may I be used in any way you choose
Because it was for your glory I was created and reserved to be used

To you, Lord, my body I bring
O God please take what is left of me, Lord to you, my heart sing
I am just a broken vessel in this divine plan
And I am so glad that it is non-negotiable and not left up to man

I know others were worthy, and that was not hard for you to find,
I still cannot fully understand it because of the frailty of my mind

Lord, O Lord, I humble myself to be used as an offering
My body is yours do whatever you please
For I was created for this purpose, and my soul agrees

WEEK 24

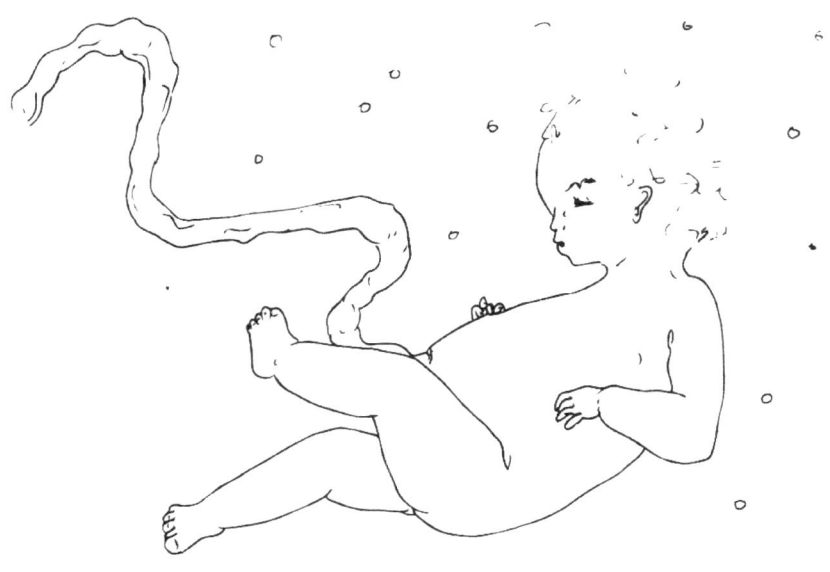

I am about the size of an ear of corn.

11.81in/30cm long

Thy hands have made me and fashioned me:

Psalm 119:17a

Dear Mom,

This week you are a little bit chubbier than your usual self. Your body is less defined because I am getting bigger and you are getting bigger. I really owe you big time Mom. I am almost 9 inches long and more than 1 pound. I am fully forming my own footprints and fingerprints, and they are unique to me. I still cannot fathom that there is no one in the whole wide world that has my footprints and fingerprints. I am continuing to be a special little one…. Mom. This week is the start of me gaining at least 6 ounces each week. My weight is a mass of fat and muscles and bones and everything that I need to be big and strong. I think I see some tiny things growing right near my eyes. Oh my! They are my eyelashes and eyebrows. I told you I am getting ready for my photoshoot. Laugh out loud! The big thing that is happening this week is that my taste, touch and all my senses are getting in sync as I am getting ready to live in your world. This is really a big deal for me. I truly appreciate you carrying me inside of you. Have I told you lately that I love you? I feel so special to call you, my mom.

Dear Child,

I find myself wanting to be frustrated by the pushing, the stretching, and the squeezing you are making inside my womb. But I cannot be frustrated, because you are mine. I love you and I want what is best in life for you. So, carry on my little child. Your little mommy is quite 'okay' with the temporary discomfort. I know your little house is getting really tight and you are trying to find space. No pressure…for the journey is coming to an end. Look at the bright side, your movements signal that there is life. The master designer is still caring for you. This week I am choosing to believe that my temporary discomfort is only for a season. I will not complain. I will embrace it because every season has its own blessings. Because of you, in this season of my life I truly can say that I am blessed. *"Weeping may endure for a night, but joy cometh in the morning"* (Psalm 30:5, KJV). Awake my child, sense His joy and His peace. Rejoice in the Lord always and again I say rejoice.

Dear Children,

"So God created man in his own image, in the image of God created he him; male and female created he them. And God blessed them,………." (Genesis

1:27-28a, KJV). You were blessed immediately after being created. Your Heavenly Father did not even consider your future failures and habits of resisting His voice…………He blessed you. A stamp of approval was placed on you. You are on this journey because we were strategically chosen by heaven. There is no surprise or coincidence in God's working space. His craftsmanship does not have a surprise element. Therefore, your blessings were not accidentally sent to another address. Your Heavenly Father knows where you are and is intimately involved in your life. Your blessings have been tailored to suit your life. That means you are not an afterthought. The intentionality of your existence is layered with your Heavenly Father's unconditional love and keen attention to the details of your life. The intricacies of this birthing experience are by far outside humans' ability to fathom the greatness of The Almighty. Despite the gap between divinity and humanity, The Holy One stepped in and bridged the gulf with His unfailing love. He started this journey bounded by a covenant that assures us that He will bless you and your offspring. Rest in the infallible words of your Heavenly Father. *"God is not a man, that he should lie; Neither the son of man, that he should repent: Hath he said, and shall he not do it? Or hath he spoken, and shall he not make it good? Behold, I have received commandment to bless: And he hath blessed; and I cannot reverse it"* (Numbers 23:19-20, KJV). You are blessed! Your blessing has been issued from the moment you were created. Your blessing has been contracted by heaven. It is signed and sealed by the hands of your Heavenly Father.

WEEK 25

I am about the size of an acorn squash.

13.62in/34.6cm long

*But now, O Lord, thou art our
father; we are the clay, and thou
our potter; and we all are the
work of thy hand.*

Isaiah 64:8

Dear Mom,

All my breathing 'tools' are getting ready for me to use them independently when I enter your world. My nose and lungs are getting up to par as well as the coating of my tiny alveoli. This week, I am spending most of my days finding ways to comfortably relax in your womb. I am so uniquely special that there has to be a force that is orchestrating all my changes in this journey. My heart is programmed to beat twice as many times as yours. It is such a wonderful thing to hear my heartbeat. Bum, bum, bum, bum. That is my heart, Mom. I am alive and I am getting ready to head your way. I am heads over heels with your love for someone that you have never met. You are the epitome of genuine love. I cannot wait to meet you.

Dear Child,

I cannot begin to tell you how much I love you. I cannot begin to tell you how much I TRULY LOVE YOU. Yet, my love for you cannot be compared with the love that our Heavenly Father has for both of us. I love you but The Divine One loves us to the extent that He gave His life for us. I love you, yet my love can be questioned. But His love cannot be questioned. He gave the ultimate sacrifice of a life so that we can have life more abundantly. I love you, but I am still learning what true love really means. He loved us despite the fact he knew that we were not perfect. But He chose to love us. Let us reflect on His love. This journey has so many footprints of love.

Dear Children,

Let your Heavenly Father's peace permeate your innermost being. Use this journey as a reminder to grow in peace—*a type of peace that is not dictated by external circumstances.* It is a type of peace that is not disturbed by problems and challenges. This peace results from disciplining your emotions to resist the habit of responding to every hiccup and unexpected situation. On this journey, many individuals find it hard to acknowledge their need for a central place where they can find peace. However, you have been on a path, and you are realizing every day the need for peace. Use this realization to strengthen your faith and to guard your mind from wallowing in the muck of anxiety and fear. On this journey, you will realize that the areas of your perceived strengths are irrelevant, and your weaknesses are obvious. This acknowledgment of this truth will draw you closer to the God who will give you His peace. *"Peace I leave with you, my peace I give unto you: not as the world giveth, give I unto you. Let not your heart be troubled, neither let it be afraid"* (John 14:27, KJV). As you take this journey in strides, you will discover that peace is not a *product*. It is not the end of a journey or a destination. You will discover that peace is a **process** of trusting and acknowledging your need for the Master. You will learn that this peace will motivate you to thank your Heavenly Father for the tough times and difficult situations. There is no need to run around being frantic about the challenges of this journey. *Challenges are interwoven into the fabric of life.* Yet there is a peace that buffers the bumps and cushions your heart to rest in God's promises. *"Be careful for nothing; but in every thing by prayer and supplication with thanksgiving let your requests be made known unto God. AND the peace of God, which passeth all understanding, shall keep your hearts and minds through Christ Jesus"* (Philippians 4:6-7, KJV). Rest in the master planner's promises. You are in the hands of a Heavenly Father who is always there to shield your mind from becoming intoxicated by the fears of life. *"For this God is our God for ever and ever: He will be our guide even unto death"* (Psalm 48:14, KJV).

WEEK 26

I am about the size of a long zucchini.

14.02in/35.6cm long

In whose hand is the soul of every living thing, and the breath of all mankind.

Job 12:10

Dear Mom,

Mom, this is our first week in the second phase of our journey together. I weigh just under 2 pounds but I am developing in accordance with The Master Designer's plan. My gymnastic skills are getting better as I can stretch out my arms and legs with such great flexibility. For the most part though, I spend my time curled up with my feet tightly tucked under my bottom. Since my eyelids are no longer tightly closed, I have been taking peeks into your womb and oh Mom, *The Master Designer created you with intricate wires and tubes on the inside* (that is my baby-term for the veins and the different body systems). Your amniotic fluid is far less during this stage of our journey and that is okay, but remember that every move I make, you are going to feel them. I will try to kick less because I do not want to hurt you. I do not intend to hurt you…...I am just excited to use these beautiful limbs that have been given to me. By the way, I have been packing on extra fat that will serve as insulation at birth. Mom, the design plan for my development has been mapped out perfectly. This cannot be the result of some haphazard events. The pieces of the puzzle are coming together. There is a master designer behind all of this…...Mom please get to know Him and promise me that you will not forget to introduce me to Him.

Dear Child,

I am conscious of our master designer's presence. I am fixated on the divine script that declares *"….and your life is hid with Christ IN God"* (Colossians 3: 3b, KJV). No evil can come near you, unless it comes through the double 'protectorship' of both our Heavenly Father and Jesus Christ. They both must remove themselves to allow danger to touch you—and that they cannot do. They are immutable; they CANNOT fail. You my child are in Christ, who is in God. Therefore, special protection is gifted to you as an honorary citizen of His Kingdom. If you and I miss out on this truth, we will feel the drudgery of this journey. On the days when I do not feel peachy, my human nature is defaulted to complaining. But I chose to remind myself that you and I are covered under a divine plan. The greatest fear that plague humanity is the fear of uncertainty. The *what ifs* are crippling. The fear of being unsafe is by far the greatest fear we encounter. Knowing that you are hidden in Christ **IN** God decreases my proclivity to worry about your wellbeing. Rest child…..The God of Jacob is our fortress and refuge- He is with us.

Dear Children,

Resting in your Heavenly Father's promises requires strength to discipline your mind to believe and trust in the holy manuscript—God's word. Your mind has the tendency to wander in the unknown and oftentimes it is when you allow this uncontrolled drifting of your thoughts that you become anxious. It is normal to think about the unknown things such as how you will fund a particular project or recover some losses that you have experienced. You may even allow your mind to explore the challenges that are typically associated with this life-event. The danger lies not within the freedom to let your thoughts drift, but rather in anchoring your wonderings on things that you cannot control. Trying to direct the uncontrollable aspects of life is a recipe for anxiety. The origin of anxiety and fears is distrust in your Heavenly Father's providence. Your Heavenly Father is the creator of all things. Not only does He create but He also sustains and nurtures that which He has created. *"Thou, even thou, art LORD alone; thou hast made heaven, the heaven of heavens, with all their host, the earth, and all things that are therein, the seas, and all that is therein, and thou preservest them all; ...."* (Nehemiah 9: 6a, KJV). The interjection of fear into your heart is lurking around to disconnect you from your Heavenly Father's plans for your life. You will only appreciate God's providential care when you dismiss your habits to question how you are going to cope with the challenges of life. Every time this habit surfaces, declare with confidence the truth that *"....God hath not given us the spirit of fear; but of power, and of love, and of a sound mind"* (2 Timothy 1:7, KJV). Embrace this truth. Until this habit of drifting into the unknown is totally eradicated, speak into the atmosphere this truth. Use it as an antidote against fear. Declare this truth until your thoughts are defaulted to trust the providential care of your Heavenly Father.

WEEK 27

I am about the size of a cauliflower.

14.41in/36.6cm long

And the Lord thy God will make thee plenteous in every work of thine hand, in the fruit of thy body, and in the fruit of thy cattle, and in the fruit of thy land, for good:

Deuteronomy 30: 9a

Dear Mom,

My house, which was so big, is getting too small for me. This week, you are going to feel me bracing on the wall of your womb. I am just trying to get my little house to expand and create space for me to live for the rest of the journey. I know it feels as if I am punching and kicking you, but I promise that I am not. I would never hurt you, Mom. I am truly trying to create a little more space here. This week, I am quickly growing and gaining fat deposits around my organs and under my skin. I am about 15 inches long, but I am curled up at times so that I do not put too much pressure on you. A quick update Mom….I have learned to soothe myself by sucking my thumb and sometimes my toes. My days are being spent using my lungs to breathe in and out the amniotic fluid. I am getting prepared to independently breathe in your world. This journey is nothing short of a miracle. I am a tiny ball of life; specially packaged by a master designer.

Dear Child,

My child, let us not lose faith in the master designer. *"The other disciples therefore said unto him, We have seen the Lord. But he (Thomas) said unto them, Except I shall see in his hands the print of the nails, and put my finger into the print of the nails, and thrust my hand into his side, I will not believe"* (John 20: 25, KJV). This journey, my child, requires faith. A few weeks ago, your existence was merely a microscopic form. There were times when I was unsure if you existed. To be truthful, there were days when I wondered if you were………But this week, I am centering my focus on The Master Designer. I will retrain my tendencies of doubt. This week, I need the stronghold of doubt to be brought down under the governance of the Holy Spirit. I do not want to be on this journey and miss that the master designer is present with us. My little one, I do not need all the details to believe that He is!

Dear Children,

The problem of life is not the problem. *The problem is that you have made the problem become your life.* There is nowhere in this universe that there is never a situation that does not have the capacity to try to work against the purpose for our lives. The problem however, arises when your mindset gets in the gear to work in opposition to the situation. When you begin to center your focus on who governs the universe and the situations within this sphere called life, you will become more aware that the situation is under HIS governance. Your ability or lack thereof to control things is the problem. In fact, it is oftentimes your quest to control your situations that creates the problem and results in things spiraling out of control. Use this journey as a stopping point on your desire to interfere with your Heavenly Father's plans for your life. Let this journey be recorded in history as the decision point to relinquish the reins and allow your Heavenly Father to reign on the throne of your heart. Your strong suggestions and proposed agendas are creating waves of problems that are impacting your life. Let go and LET GOD! Let go of what you cannot control and embrace the change of rulership over your life. Use this journey to inaugurate The King of Kings and The Lord of Lords as the only ruling power in your life. Give Him access to fulfill His purpose for your life. *"Trust in the LORD with all thine heart; And lean not unto thine own understanding. In all thy ways acknowledge him, And he shall direct thy paths. Be not wise in thine own eyes: ………….."* (Proverbs 3:5-7a, KJV).

WEEK 28

I am about the size of an eggplant.

14.80in/37.6cm long

By thee have I been holden up from the womb: thou art he that took me out of my mother's bowels: my praise shall be continually of thee.

Psalm 71: 6

Dear Mom,

This week is pretty much a practice drill of breathing amniotic fluid in and out my lungs. Just a heads-up Mom, I am getting some sleep which is beneficial for my brain development. My brain is also getting many grooves on the surface. Amazing work of art! I am not sure, but this week I may be getting my own toupée—*I told you that I am getting ready for my photoshoot.* By the way, you are going to be tinkling a lot more this week. I have been hanging out on top of your bladder. If you lay on your side, I will try my best to move to another section of my cozy home.

Dear Child,

Your existence is bonded by an everlasting covenant. *"So shall my word be that goeth forth out of my mouth: it shall not return unto me void, but it shall accomplish that which I please, and it shall prosper in the thing whereto I sent it"* (Isaiah 55: 11, KJV). His word started this journey- and God's word MUST accomplish that which it was set forth to perform. I cannot begin to fully understand the surety of His words. *"Heaven and earth shall pass away, but my words shall not pass away"* (Matthew 24: 35, KJV). The master designer is particular about His words. You, my child is a fruit of His word. Our Heavenly Father has made a covenant with you. His word will not and cannot return to Him void (not accomplishing its intent). During the week of creation, He spoke every detail into being by the use of His Word. Oh little one, during the week of creation it was ten times that God said….Let there be AND there was. His words are our blank check. You and I are protected by His words.

Dear Children,

"By the word of the LORD were the heavens made; And all the host of them by the breath of his mouth" (Psalm 33:6, KJV). This journey should be an opportunity to spend time in your Heavenly Father's presence. As you spend time in His presence you will begin craving His words. Your appetite for His presence will be insatiable. God's word has creative power to bring things into existence. It is His ruach (breath) that gives life to everything. *"Thus saith the Lord GOD unto these bones; Behold, I will cause breath to enter into you, and ye shall live: and I will lay sinews upon you, and will bring up flesh upon you, and cover you with skin, and put breath in you, and ye shall*

live; and ye shall know that I am the LORD." (Ezekiel 37:5-6, KJV). Use this as an opportunity to note the areas in your life that need to be resuscitated. Give your Heavenly Father permission to blow His Spirit into those areas. Remove the **Do N**ot **R**esuscitate (DNR) sign from those areas of your life. Segmenting your life into different compartments while restricting your Heavenly Father from entering these forbidden zones are signs of '**SELF-CONTROL**'—*not the ability to regulate yourself but the pushback to accept your Heavenly Father to control you.* Remove the caution tape and allow the breath of your Heavenly Father to restore and make YOU whole. This journey speaks to the credibility of a master designer who is qualified to infuse life into situations that the human mind cannot comprehend. He can see the entire picture and bring pieces of the puzzle into focus. *"And he that searcheth the hearts knoweth what is the mind of the Spirit, because he maketh intercession for the saints according to the will of God. And we know that all things work together for good to them that love God, to them who are the called according to his purpose"* (Romans 8: 27-28, KJV).

WEEK 29

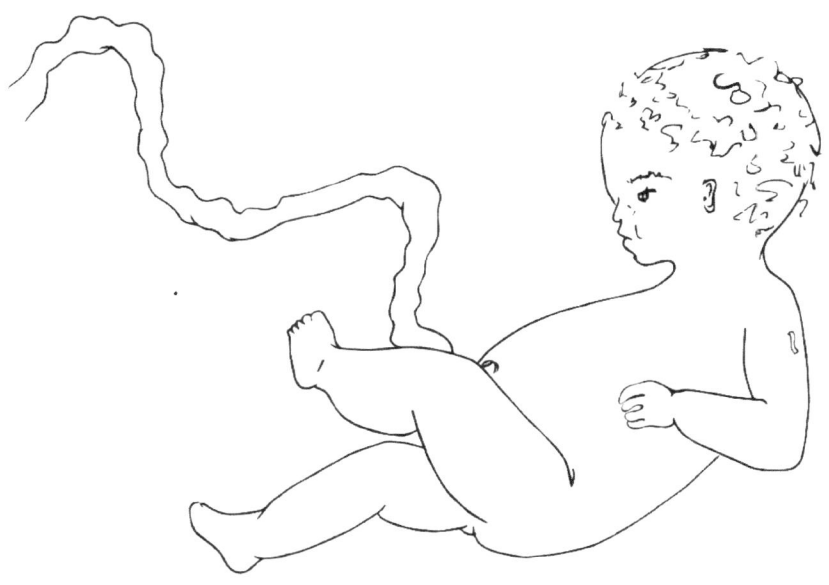

I am about the size of a butternut squash.

15.02in/38.6cm long

And now, saith the Lord that formed me from the womb to be his servant, to bring Jacob again to him, Though Israel be not gathered, yet shall I be glorious in the eyes of the Lord, and my God shall be my strength.

Isaiah 49:5

Dear Mom,

This week I may be a little more agitated if anyone pushes too hard on your belly. It is not too much drama. At this stage of the journey, my protective instincts are fired up because the master designer has shown me how to insulate myself. I know that you are waddling like a duck to carry the weight of your pregnancy, however, I still think that you are absolutely beautiful. By the way, my airways are developing, and the tree-like structures (alveoli and bronchioles) are multiplying. I am reaching another milestone with the volume of fat deposits under my skin, but I am still a little over a half of my birth weight. I am definitely in awe at the wonders of this divine masterpiece........*from a fertilized egg to an embryo*. Amazing!

Dear Child,

Pregnancy is not an easy feat. My dear baby, pregnancy requires grit. There are good days and bad days. There are times even on a 'good' day that I feel less than peachy. Sometimes, I am not sure what are *good days* versus *bad days*. However, I am sure that our Heavenly Father knows about the complexities of carrying you. I am reminded that our Heavenly Father never promised us a comfortable life. However, what He has promised is that His grace is sufficient to keep me. *"And he said unto me, my grace is sufficient for thee: for my strength is made perfect in weakness. Most gladly therefore will I rather glory in my infirmities, that the power of Christ may rest upon me"* (1 Corinthians 12: 9, KJV). When I read that in the divine script my dear child, I became joyful to bear the ups and downs of this journey. To carry you is a moment in time when earthly beings get to work alongside heaven. Oh what honor! My dearest one, I am not bothered by this temporary 'inconvenience'—*this too will pass*. Rest sleepy one, you are loved.

Dear Children,

Your efforts to understand all the intricacies of this journey is futile. Your academic achievements pales in the presence of the power that is at work. When compared to the true source of power, your strengths are weaknesses packaged in human intelligence. *"I know that thou canst do every thing, And that no thought can be withholden from thee"* (Job 42:2, KJV). The intricacies of this journey are beyond human comprehension, and the wisdom of humanity has no place in this divine transaction. Your involvement in this journey should be an applause of praise. Your life should be layered with intimate worship. What doubts are still lingering in your mind regarding the sovereignty of your Heavenly Father? His jurisdiction is heaven and earth. Open your mouth and utter worship to your God. *"I will bless the LORD at all times: His praise shall continually be in my mouth. My soul shall make her boast in the LORD: The humble shall hear thereof, and be glad. O magnify the LORD with me, And let us exalt his name together"* (Psalm 34:1-3, KJV). Your praise will rise when you become aware of the fact that your journey is God-ordained. Your Heavenly Father is the master designer of all the details contained in this experience. Your doctor's input is limited by the constraints of human frailties and therefore should not take precedence over your Heavenly Father's guidance. Begin spending time in His presence so you will become acquainted with His voice. Mute the noise around you and enter a sacred place where His presence can become your home. Seek not His presence to become powerful, rather seek after Him to reflect His character. His wisdom does not come from taking counsel from human sources. This journey is a product of The Godhead and you are a recipient of divinity. *"Praise ye the LORD. I will praise the LORD with my whole heart,…..,. The works of the LORD are great, Sought out of all them that have pleasure therein. His work is honourable and glorious: And his righteousness endureth for ever. He hath made his wonderful works to be remembered: The LORD is gracious and full of compassion. He hath given meat unto them that fear him: He will ever be mindful of his covenant"* (Psalm 111:1a-5, KJV). Use this journey as a pit stop to refuel your awareness of your Heavenly Father's majesty. Become more attuned to His presence and the *God-whispers* that He speaks in your innermost being. *"For I know that the LORD is great, And that our Lord is above all gods. Whatsoever the LORD pleased, that did he in heaven, and in earth, in the seas, and all deep places"* (Psalm 135:5-6, KJV).

WEEK 30

I am about the size of a cabbage.

15.71in/39.9cm long

Thus saith the Lord that made thee, and formed thee from the womb, which will help thee; Fear not, O Jacob, my servant;

Isaiah 44: 2a

Dear Mom,

Mom, the countdown for my entrance into your world has begun. We are now more than 75% of this wonderful journey. This week I am approximately 17 inches long and I am nearing the 4 pounds marker. The loose skin on my body is filling out with fat. It seems that I have my own personal plastic surgeon living here with me. I am getting my own tummy-tucks and butt-cheeks lifts. Laugh out loud! By the way, my brain and nervous system are almost fully mature. At birth I will have millions of neurons for you to stimulate with your loving connections which will help to form the synapses and link the neurons. Please do not forget that you can start communicating with me. I am definitely a sucker for your voice and happy laughter. My days of somersaulting are dwindling because the space in my little one-bedroom house is crammed. That is okay, because I am coming home to you!

Dear Child,

I am counting down the days yet silently wishing that the sacred time with the master design would never end. I am resting in the knowledge that His grace is sufficient to keep me. I am rehearsing His promises recorded in the divine script.

(1) *"Fear thou not; for I am with thee: be not dismayed; for I am thy God: I will strengthen thee; yea, I will help thee; yea, I will uphold thee with the right hand of my righteousness"* (Isaiah 41:10, KJV).

(2) *"When thou passest through the waters, I will be with thee; and through the rivers, they shall not overflow thee: when thou walkest through the fire, thou shalt not be burned; neither shall the flame kindle upon thee"* (Isaiah 43: 2, KJV).

(3) *"For the Lord God is a sun and shield: the Lord will give grace and glory: no good thing will he withhold from them that walk uprightly"* (Psalm 84:11, KJV).

(4) *"And the Lord, he it is that doth go before thee; he will be with thee, he will not fail thee, neither forsake thee: fear not, neither be dismayed"* (Deuteronomy 31: 8, KJV).

Oh dear child, the divine script is filled with the master designer's promises. Yes, my little one, we can trust His words. *"God is not a man, that he should lie; neither the son of man, that he should repent: hath he said, and shall he not do it? or hath he spoken, and shall he not make it good?"* (Numbers 23: 19, KJV). His promises are true. On this journey and through eternity we can trust Him. *"The Lord is not slack concerning his promise, as some men count slackness; but is longsuffering to us-ward, not willing that any should perish...."* (2 Peter 3: 9, KJV). Oh what peace we sometimes forfeit simply because we fail to trust Him. My dear child, trust Him!

Dear Children,

At this stage of the journey, you should be more open to accepting His plans for your life. Your tendency to give pushbacks and to control your life should begin dissipating. This time of diminishing self should give birth in you a desire to anchor your confidence in a God who cannot fail. The longer you practice the habit of surrendering your will to your Heavenly Father the easier you will default to trust. You will begin discovering that trusting your Heavenly Father results in an inner peace. Your situation may not have changed but your perspective has been realigned. You are becoming more attuned to His will for your life. *"For I know the thoughts that I think toward you, saith the LORD, thoughts of peace, and not of evil, to give you an expected end. THEN shall ye call upon me, and ye shall go and pray unto me, and I will hearken unto you. And ye shall seek me, and find me, when ye shall search for me with all your heart. AND I will be found of you, saith the LORD: ......"* (Jeremiah 29:11-14a, KJV). Your Heavenly Father's plans for you have been explicitly stated. Consequently, there is a response that is required of you, and that is for you to call upon Him and seek Him. Heaven is already waiting to reciprocate this gesture....... *"AND I will be found of you, saith the LORD: ......"* (Jeremiah 29: 14a, KJV). Let this journey be a season of restoring your confidence in knowing that your Heavenly Father knows what is best for you. Let your squirming and pushing against His will begin to fade. Enter a new phase of your life when praying *"not my will Lord but thy will be done"* becomes an expression of your heart. At this stage of the journey, you should begin sensing that the intricacies of this life-experience is beyond human comprehension. At this point you will begin to discover that the doctors and specialists are now reading from a medical script that is merely based on suggestions and hypothetical scenarios. On the contrary, your Heavenly Father KNOWS and is orchestrating all the changes. This masterpiece is yet another wondrous display of a heavenly experience!

WEEK 31

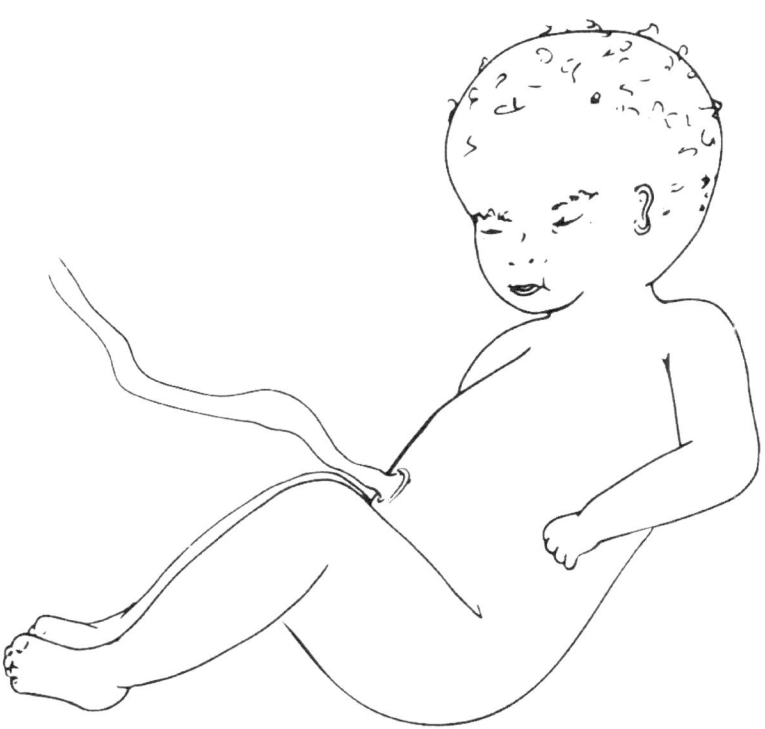

I am about the size of a coconut.

16.18in/41.1cm long

Can a woman forget her sucking child, that she should not have compassion on the son of her womb? yea, they may forget, yet will I not forget thee. Behold, I have graven thee upon the palms of my hands…

Isaiah 49:15 & 16a

Dear Mom,

Yippee Mom! I am only 3 inches less than my typical birth length and my weight is increasing. You can blame this rapid growth on the benefits of taking extended periods of **R**apid **E**ye **M**ovement (REM) sleep. The master designer has scheduled my brain and complex nerve development for this week. Your voice Mom, the music and sounds from your world are causing the synapses in my brain to be formed by the millions. This week you can continue to think about what life will be when I enter your world but remember that it is The Master Designer who is in control. As my birth is getting closer, you are going to spend more time thinking about our life together. For me, our life together has already begun. My birth will only be a continuation of our *love-bond*. I really love you Mom! I am beaming with joy to see your reaction when you meet me. It has been such a holy moment to live inside a woman who embraces and carries me. I am indeed loved.

Dear Child,

I find myself wanting to be frustrated by the pushing and the stretching and the squeezing you are making inside. However, I cannot be because you are mine. I love you and I want the best for you. So, carry on my little child. Your little mommy is quite okay with her continued temporary discomfort. I know your little house is getting really tight in there and you are trying to find space, but the journey is coming to an end. Look at the bright side……. Your movements signal the sacredness of life. Undoubtedly, the master designer is still caring for you. This week I am choosing to believe that my discomfort is a part of the orchestrated blueprint. and our Heavenly Father will not give me more than I can bear. I will not spend precious time 'praying' it away. I will embrace it because every season has its own blessing. In this season of my life I have been living a life of favor and blessings—*it is a reward for carrying you my child*!

Dear Children,

This is a journey that confirms your Heavenly Father consistencies. Despite your unreliable hormonal documentation (the days when you feel under the weather and crushed by the weight of life's pressure), heaven has an accurate record that notates your **NEVER**s. Your Heavenly Father has

never left you alone, **never** forsaken you, **never** abandoned you, **never** given up on you, never sent your blessings to the wrong house address, **never** ignored you, or **never** withhold His love from you. Your **NEVER**s is a good stopping point that you can use to remember all your unsolicited blessings. These *automated-blessings* are consistently poured out without measure. Without measure means there is no measuring system to calculate the amount that you are receiving. Your blessings are without limitations, without boundaries, and without parameters. Your Heavenly Father has just opened the floodgates and sent an untapped number of blessings. *"Bring ye all the tithes into the storehouse, that there may be meat in mine house, and prove me now herewith, saith the LORD of hosts, if I will not open you the windows of heaven, and pour you out a blessing, that there shall not be room enough to receive it. And I will rebuke the devourer for your sakes, and he shall not destroy the fruits of your ground; neither shall your vine cast her fruit before the time in the field, saith the LORD of hosts. And all nations shall call you blessed: for ye shall be a delightsome land, saith the LORD of hosts"* (Malachi 3:10-12 KJV). This firsthand declaration from the mouth of God (saith The Lord of Hosts) is backed by heaven. Your **NEVER**s are sure. You will not only be a recipient of blessings, but you will also be called blessed by your community of onlookers. Do not for one minute equate this type of blessing with only financial currency. You are blessed in areas that surpass extrinsic wealth. Your existence and capacity to walk this journey are signs of a blessed life. The breath of life that circulates through your body is a blessing beyond human reasoning. Look beyond your disappointments and challenges and come to an awakening that despite the fact that life is riddled with pain— *you are still blessed!* Being blessed does not mean there is an absence of struggles. A blessed life is not excluded from heartaches nor is it protected from suffering. A blessed life belongs to someone who respects each season of life and honors the experiences as trophies worthy of telling a story. In this journey diligently seek out ways to celebrate your life for what it is worth to your Heavenly Father. What if your blessings come through teardrops?

WEEK 32

I am about the size of a jicama.

16.19in/42.4cm long

Remember the former things of old: for I am God, and there is none else; I am God, and there is none like me, Declaring the end from the beginning, and from ancient times the things that are not yet done, saying, My counsel shall stand, and I will do all my pleasure:

Isaiah 46: 9-10

Dear Mom,

We are officially in the 8th month of our journey together. This week I am just under 9 inches long and a little less than 4 pounds. I am gaining approximately one-half pound this week. I am about to enter into your world, and I have to be ready for my big photoshoot. I am perfecting my kicking, sucking, swallowing and frowning skills. Moving my head side to side and opening and closing my eyes is a breeze! My little house is getting very crammed and so you are going to feel me touching your sides. This is a very busy week for me, but I am finding time to take long periods of sleep. Please make sure you are getting sufficient sleep because when I enter your world, I may keep you awake at nights. My week is going to be filled with getting my bones calcified which is pretty hard by the date of my birth, and I will be getting some fat injected under my skin. This is definitely a journey of a lifetime. Mom, oh Mom, are you amazed as I am?

Dear Child,

Oh Lord, you are the potter, and I am the clay. So, mold me and form me in accordance with your will—this is my daily prayer. I am praying for both of us, my dear child. We are in the hands of the master designer, and He has the capacity to mold us and form us into what He wants us to be. I am praying today, my child, that I will be pliable in His hands so that He can mold me and teach me how to reflect His glory. One of the responsibilities of carrying you is that I am required to teach you while you are in my womb to love righteousness. I am giving myself to the Divine One so that the byproduct of my submission to Him is that you will be the recipient of His' blessings. I pray that this week I will submit my will to Him. As the day grows closer to your delivery date, I realize that the responsibilities of parenting never end. I am teaching you while you are in my womb, so take note and trust that I am learning from the greatest teacher whoever ever walked this earth. There are areas in my life where I am broken, so I am praying each day that the potter will mend me and use me in His service. During this journey, I want Him to pour His Holy Spirit in me, so that as I carry you, you will sense His glory and the power of His anointing. My child, this journey requires complete submission of **self**. Let me quickly tell you my sweet child, it is painful to submit. However, to be a good mom that teaches you the ways of the Lord requires me to submit my will, and my ways, and to let Him lead me in the path of righteousness.

Dear Children,

On this journey, the fiery attacks on your soul and mind will ever be so present. The more time that you spend in your Heavenly Father's presence, the more the forces of evil will attach themselves to your mind. The evil one will have a field day in your thoughts. You will find yourself having to speak God's words openly and loudly. This battle for the mind is in full swing because you are detoxing your life from things that do not glorify God. You are also becoming more aware of the people in your inner circle who are not depositing in your spiritual bank. Your stance on this journey is causing the evil forces to come against you. *"For we wrestle not against flesh and blood, but against principalities, against powers, against the rulers of the darkness of this world, against spiritual wickedness in high places"* (Ephesians 6: 12, KJV). At this stage of this journey, you are becoming more divinely attuned that you have been entrusted with a living soul. In this transaction, you are the direct link between heaven and earth. **The desire to please SELF is diminishing and you are now required to forfeit your Me-agenda.** *"Submit yourselves therefore to God. Resist the devil, and he will flee from you. Draw nigh to God, and he will draw nigh to you"* (James 4: 7-8, KJV). Do not engage in this battle for the mind. Physical beings cannot defeat spirit beings. Resist the urge to flex your muscles or display your SELF-moves. The evil one knows that you are no match for him. Rather, call upon your Heavenly Father. He is the real deal and the evil one knows! Remember that this battle was already won at Calvary's cross, so this is a re-run! Jesus Christ already defeated the devil at the cross. The adversary was having a field day when they were mocking Jesus as He hung from the cross. The joke ended when the soldiers pierced Jesus' side and His blood spilled. **The shedding of Jesus' blood settled the score.** So, as you encounter these intensified challenges, reflect on the cross. This journey and its avalanche of problems are a part of what Jesus' death settled. Reassess your connection to the power source. Ensure that you are directly plugged into your Heavenly Father's power outlet. Ensure that your wires (YOU) are not tangled by anything that can disrupt the flow of power. Heaven is standing at alert and waiting to be dispatched to fight on your behalf. *"Ah Lord God! behold, thou hast made the heaven and the earth by thy great power and stretched out arm, and there is nothing too hard for thee:......... the Great, the Mighty God, the Lord of hosts, is his name. Great in counsel, and mighty in work: ...."* (Jeremiah 32: 17,18b- 19a KJV). You are in good hands. Your God is mighty in battle. Get out of your Heavenly Father's way. He is here to defend you. Do not interfere in what He is doing nor interject yourself in His battle. Thus saith the Lord unto you, *"Be not afraid nor dismayed by reason of this great multitude; for the battle is not yours, but God's"* (2 Chronicles 20:15, KJV).

IF ONLY I KNEW

Looking back at the decisions I made

They would have been aligned to my purpose only if I knew the reason that I came

All the rebellion and detours I took

If only I knew that my purpose was already in The Book

I look back Lord and cringe at what I thought was just life's game

So, I throw myself at your feet Lord because there is no one to blame

My purpose was already created before I was even a thought

No wonder your son came Lord and for me salvation was wrought

He took the nails in His hands and the sword plunged in His side

Because He knew my purpose, He removed my excuses, so I dare not hide

So, use my body Lord to carry your breath

Because it was for me Lord you suffered a cruel death

This child that I bear Lord belongs to you

And I am simply a vessel that is willing to be used

Thanks for including me in this awesome plan

If this is my purpose Lord, then let it be done

WEEK 33

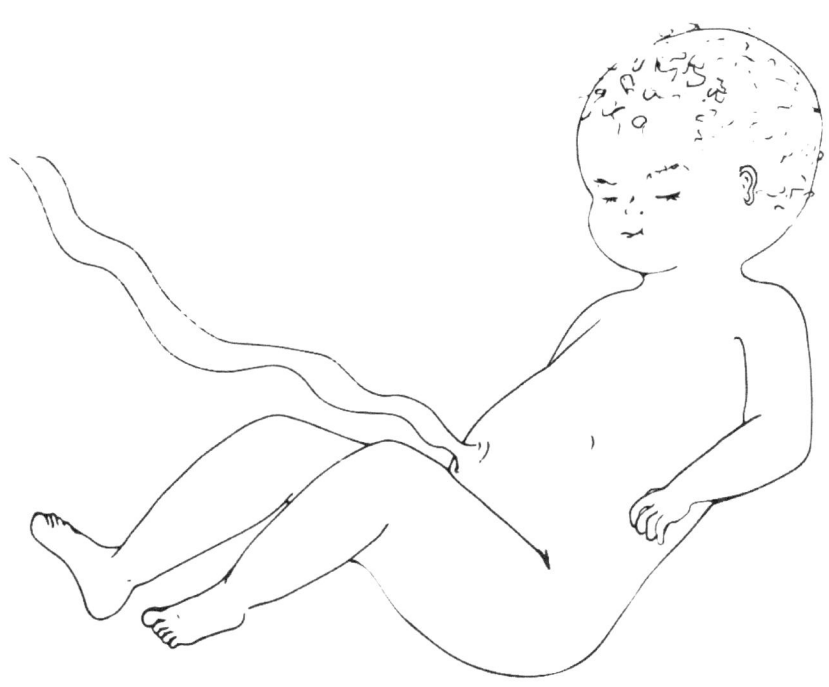

I am about the size of a pineapple.

17.20in/43.7cm long

Even so it is not the will of your Father which is in heaven, that one of these little ones should perish.

Matthew 18: 14

Dear Mom,

Mom, you are fully pregnant! Everything about you is about me. People are no longer interested in asking about you…It is all about ME! This week, my journey is focused on the maturation of my lungs. My little body is making enough surfactant to keep my airways fully open. The amniotic fluid is producing in abundance, and I am having a wonderful time in this warm bath. I told you Mom, my journey is a masterpiece. The production of amniotic fluid is a sign that my kidneys are up and running. I am producing about 1 cup of amniotic fluid each day! By the way, I will be sending strong kicks and bumps your way because my house is getting really tight. What a marvelous experience!!

Dear Child,

Dear child, being pregnant is like running a marathon. It is not a sprint to the finishing line. It is long and sometimes I get so tired. In order not to be discouraged, I have to fasten my eyes on the finishing line and stay focused. Not everyone gets to be on this journey, either because they do not want to be on this journey or they have not been chosen for this journey. For whatever reason, I have been chosen to be on this journey. So, as I run this marathon, I want to be able to say *"I have fought a good fight, I have finished my course, I have kept the faith I want to finish this race"* (2 Timothy 4:7, KJV) and at the end of this journey I want to hear from the lips of the master designer *"Well done, thou good and faithful servant: thou hast been faithful over a few things, I will make thee ruler over many things:"* (Matthew 25: 21a, KJV). Whenever I get tired and feel as if my strength is failing, those are the times when I have to command my soul to trust the Divine One. Thankfully, He hears and restores my strength and reaffirms my faith in Him. Oh, my child, I am confident of this one thing, that He who hath begun a good work in you will perform it. Our Heavenly Father never shirks from His responsibilities—He never leaves a job unfinished. He is The Alpha and Omega. He is The Beginning and The End.

Dear Children,

Imagine a life that is fully entrusted in God's hands…….*that would be a life that is centered around pleasing God.* However, it does not necessarily mean that it is a squeaky clean, goody-two-shoe, never did anything wrong kind of life. Oh no! A life that is entrusted in God's care, is a life that deliberately interweaves God in every compartment of life. The truth is, you are struggling to conform to a lifestyle that is governed by your Heavenly Father. You do not mind a mixture of SELF and God, but a totally GOD living arrangement is not your style. If there was a slight chance that you would entertain this God-is-in-control lifestyle, your circle of influence would question your change in areas such as your behaviors, and you would feel pressured to explain that you are no longer governed by SELF. Would you consider requesting help from The Holy Spirit as a possibility? Then do so! *"What? know ye not that your body is the temple of the Holy Ghost which is in you, which ye have of God, and ye are not your own? For ye are bought with a price: therefore glorify God in your body, and in your spirit, which are God's"* (1 Corinthians 6: 19-20, KJV). This journey can be a place of full submission. You are carrying a living soul inside of you. The thought of a soul should be enough to awaken your senses to the revelation that the Holy Spirit wants to invade your life. A *God-centered* life is possible through the power of the Holy Spirit. What are your hindrances? If not a God-centered life, then what lifestyle are you opting for? As a participant in this journey, you at least have a knowledge of what a submitted will resembles. In fact, to come this far in the journey you have given up quite a bit of SELF to host this living soul that is inside of you. Your habit of relinquishing your agenda is being polished. Then, why not submit it ALL? *"This I say then, Walk in the Spirit, and ye shall not fulfil the lust of the flesh. For the flesh lusteth against the Spirit, and the Spirit against the flesh: and these are contrary the one to the other: so that ye cannot do the things that ye would"* (Galatians 5: 16-17, KJV). A life that is governed by God, has the authority to exercise the right to live a life of holiness. This journey is a beautiful stopping point that marks what it means to be used by God. Your body is a vessel of obedience as you carry a soul within you. A life of submission is therefore a life that allows God to disrupt the ME-agenda. *"A new heart also will I give you, and a new spirit will I put within you: and I will take away the stony heart out of your flesh, and I will give you a heart of flesh. And I will put my spirit within you, and cause you to walk in my statutes, and ye shall keep my judgments, and do them"* (Ezekiel 36: 26-27, KJV).

WEEK 34

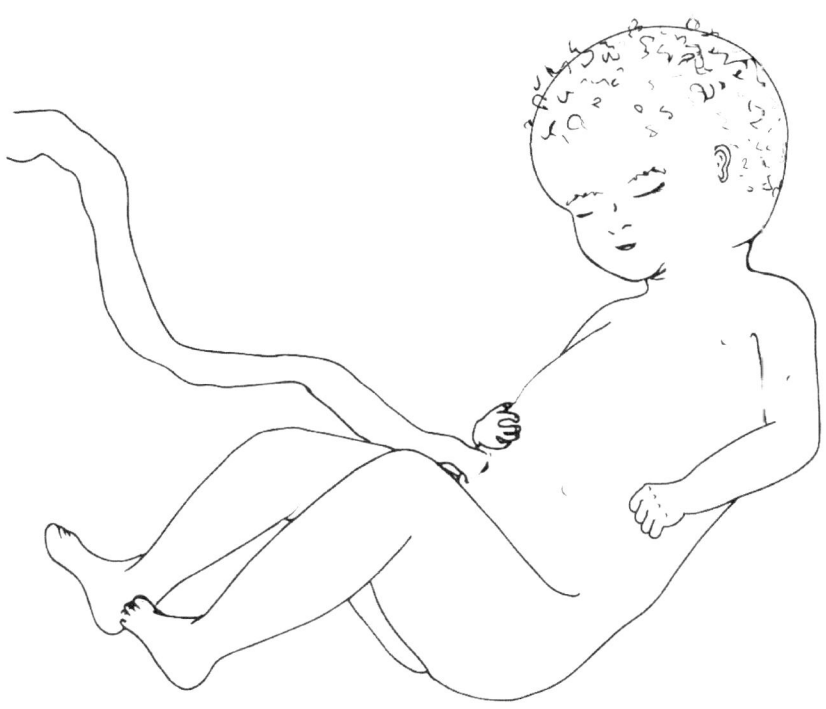

I am about the size of a cantaloupe.

17.72in/45cm long

They shall not labor in vain, nor bring forth for trouble; for they are the seed of the blessed of the Lord, and their offspring with them.

Isaiah 65: 23

Dear Mom,

My house that seemed so big at the start of our journey is now so small (you might be tired of hearing me repeat the same words). Your pregnancy hormones have made my genitals become so swollen. Not to worry, all this will be fixed at my birth. I am more attuned with my ability to open and close my eyes. This week I am spending my time practicing how to blink and focus my eyes, so I can see your beautiful face when we meet each other. Right now, bright lights are a little too much for me because I am overly sensitive to extremely stimulating things. By the way Mom, the soft hair called the lanugo that is covering my entire body is starting to disappear this week. There are a few more kinks that are being worked out so that I can independently live in your world. Right now, I am relaxing and letting the master designer finish the perfect touches to my *selfie*! My adrenal glands are communicating with my lungs to make them more surfactant, and I love being the recipient of this detailed work. Indeed, I am wonderfully made!

Dear Child,

My sweet little child, as the weeks progress, I am made aware of my need to be fully dependent on our Heavenly Father. My nature to control my life and to be in charge of my circumstances, have been stripped away. I am becoming more aware that my desire to satisfy my pride has actually stifled my growth. *Not being in control drives me nuts!* I want to be the pilot of my life. If I have to settle for a co-pilot role in my life, at least let me be able to have the items on my agenda realized. Oh no! This journey does not give me the liberty to be in control. The details, the planning, the changes are all syncing and I have nothing to do with the process!!!!!!!!!! *I, me, mine, self………..The Master Designer has thought about and executed all the details without consulting me!!!!* Oh my child, my precious child, I so badly want to be SUPER mom. But I am not! This journey is not about me and my agenda. The gift of you is so precious and He (the master designer) has not left it up to me to meddle in heavenly matters. The Holy One of Israel has placed so much value on your life and my tendency to control and oftentimes interfere has been made obsolete. My darling baby, the intricacy of your existence is not up for negotiations. It feels as if The Divine One has placed a ring of fire around you. I am yet to see another transaction that requires this amount of top security. His plans for your life started before you were even formed in my womb. I am now made aware that my need for control is a form of idolatry—*which is promoting self-desires above God's plans.* I am so sorry, my child, that I have gone the distance to attempt controlling the plans. Believe me, I just wanted to be Super Mom. As we progress in this journey, I am learning how to relinquish my 'rights' to control. My plans for my life and your life are not always in alignment with the master designer's will, and that is a major problem. So this week, I am handing over the reins, giving up the 'pilotship', firing SELF, and deleting the option of pride. Oh my child, your dear mom no longer wants to be a Super Mom. I only want to be a humble vessel that carries a precious child. Oh what a privilege to be a part of a divine plan.

Dear Children,

Your date of birth, your date of death, and a long line in between are permanent markings of a tombstone. The long line is called LIFE—your life. In this journey, God has chosen to include in your life a divine transaction between heaven and earth. Many lives are void of life. People have created a timeline for their lives, a timeline that tabulates each life event. Yet, many of them have reached a stage in life and realized that they did not include in their timeline LIVING in their life. They have aged with bank accounts that are filled with monetary gains but wishing that they could reverse the hands of the clock to include a journey like this one. They were detailed in mapping out all their lives' experiences but figured that a journey like this would be an interruption in their plans. You however, are on this journey amidst the challenges and the hiccups. Does your decision authorize you to boast about you or degrade their choices? *"The Lord thy God hath chosen thee to be a special people unto himself, above all people that are upon the face of the earth. The Lord did not set his love upon you, nor choose you, because ye were more in number than any people; for ye were the fewest of all people: But because the Lord loved you,........"* (Deuteronomy 7: 6b-8a, KJV). Your Heavenly Father rejoices over you because you have made a decision to enter a contract with heaven. Reflect on your life and see the hands of God printed all over the pages. Even in the difficult times, His footsteps are visible. In your life, there were more than enough opportunities to get despondent and give up. Yet, your Heavenly Father has walked with you in these difficult times. *The 'betterness' outweighed the bitterness.* The time called LIFE that has been given to you, is numbered and that is all that you know. How long you have been given, is the unknown. So the challenge is turning your minutes into moments. Learn how to praise your Heavenly Father in your pain. Find a message in your mess and share your testimony in the midst of your test. Do not wait for the next life's event to celebrate. A man who is 20 years old and has 2 years to live is older than a man who is 70 years old and has 30 years to live. The issue is that you cannot control your time. You cannot manage what you do not have the power to control. Let this journey be a reminder of the value of time. Live each minute with purpose! Your Heavenly Father loves you and wants to be IN your life.

FOR YOU MY CHILD

Chosen by grace, oh what a Heavenly call
My body was summoned to give its all
I was chosen by heaven to be a house of worship and praise
I am still in wonder and standing in daze

Despite my imperfections I carried a seed that was sown
I was beckoned for a purpose, and the details were unknown
Before you were even a thought my body was approved
All forces of darkness were frozen and were not allowed to move

Angelic beings were released and sent on a mission
So, you Father knew that I had no need to fear because there would be provision
O my child, I was created just for you
My assignment was signed and sealed and I had no clue

The fibers in my body were knitted together and so I had no need to fear
My purpose was unsolicited, and it was now clear
O what a sacred design
A gift of love, O my child this is truly divine.

WEEK 35

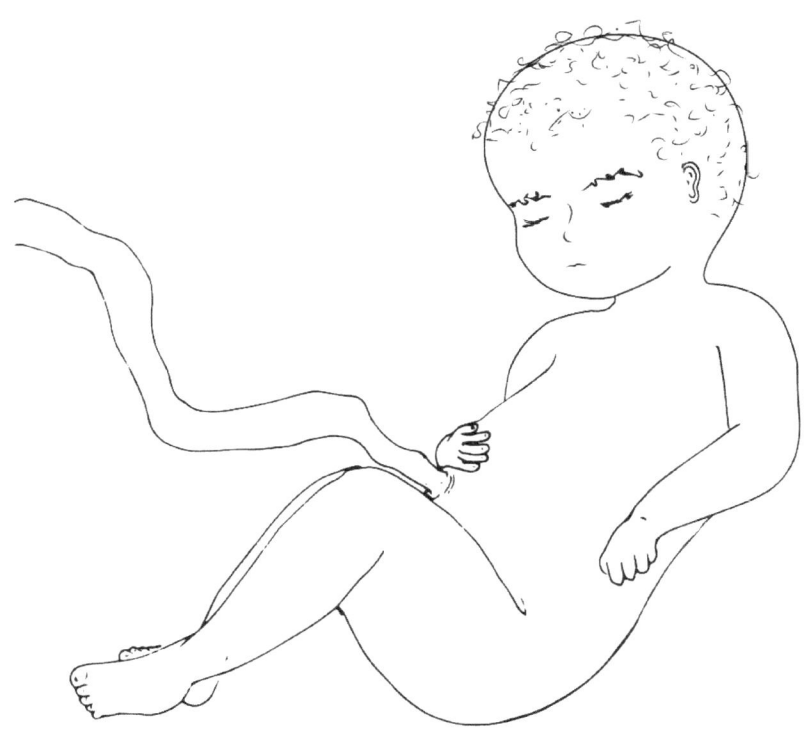

I am about the size of a honeydew melon.

18.19in/46.2cm long

*Did not he that made me in the
womb make him? and did not
one fashion us in the womb?*

Job 31:15

Dear Mom,

Mom, we are getting close to our big day. It now seems as if 9 months is not so long. This week, my brain development is booming. At this stage of the journey I will be gaining on average one pound. Considering how heavy and tired you feel, one pound might not seem much, but in babyland, one pound is a big deal. Nineteen inches and an additional one more pound of fat—superb! This week I am using most of my strength to gain more weight. I am not focused on my length since my length is basically already at my birth-length. I am not moving around as I used to, because my little house is not suitable for somersaults and gymnastics. It is crammed in here! I cannot wait to get out….I am just kidding. I am patiently waiting for my debut. My time living inside of you has been wonderful!

Dear Child,

I am humbled that I have been chosen to be your Mom. As the journey comes closer to the final days, I am still left wondering, "why me?" Why would heaven choose ME to carry you—a precious gift? It feels like my womb was used by heaven as a conduit or a vessel to bring forth a miracle. What an honor to submit my body to be used for God's glory. The challenges of carrying a child inside of me, has been outweighed by the glory that I have experienced. I feel as if I was called to enter the stage of life where a masterpiece drama is being played out before my eyes. As I entered the stage, I was only given a script that said, "Trust Me". It reminds of the story of Moses and the children of Israel at the Red Sea. *"And Moses said unto the people, Fear ye not, stand still, and see the salvation of the Lord, which he will shew to you to day…… The Lord shall fight for you, and ye shall hold your peace"* (Exodus 14: 13a & 14, KJV). It is a humbling experience to be in a scene of life and not be the 'director of the events'. I am handed the TRUST ME script with no table of contents so I can flip to the section of the script that tells me what is going to happen in the next scene. There is no addendum to suggest that the script can be altered or modified to insert my suggestions or at least my director skills. I did wish that whenever I wanted to leave the stage, that at least the script would have additional instructions on 'how do I exit the stage' because I knew that I would not like certain details of the script. Then I remember that if the master designer did provide 'cheat sheets', then, there would be no need to TRUST. The script does not offer the liberty to exit and enter the stage, and that to me erases my DNA of independence. Derived from the medieval French word, **depenre**, the word *independence* literally means to hang down or hang from. The Latin prefix *in*, renders the word independence to mean not hanging from. This creates the conversation that being independent offers freedom from control; which allows the openness to organize your own life and operate under the rulership of your guidance. Truthfully dear little one, there is no such thing as freedom. There is always something or someone that is controlling the script. When this realization was awakened in me, I arose from the depressive thought that the Divine One was controlling the script of this journey. My love, I do not want to let **SELF** be in control of this script. I want to pass on to you traits of peace—the kind of peace that passeth all understanding. This will set you up for victory in all areas of your life. Being in control diminishes peace. Being obsessed with wanting to know all the details of the script hinders my ability from resting in my Heavenly Father and accepting His will. As I walk this journey with you, my dear child, the more I am convinced that fear is a tormenting spirit. Fear has the potential to prevent you from becoming all that you were created to become. Therefore, if fear is a spirit, it has the capacity to imprison you. I do not wish for my sweet baby to operate life from a place of bondage—*being held captive by a controlling spirit.* I wish for you a life of trust and complete dependence on the Most High God. I pray that your life will be infused with faith. I pray that you will place your trust in a God that cannot and WILL NOT fail. Oh my dear child, this week I chose to celebrate the script that was handed to me—*the script that demanded my full participation in carrying you.* I relinquish my mindset and recognize that it is a privilege to carry you, and it is not a right. So grow little one and one day I hope that you will be a child that embraces the script that says— TRUST the I AM that I AM.

Dear Children,

You were created to be an emotional being, so being sad is not the end of the world. Your Heavenly Father will not punish you because you expressed emotions of sadness, nor will He be upset with you because you told everyone that you are overwhelmed and frustrated. His desire is that you would go to Him and release those feelings on Him. Do not pretend to be happy when you are not. Do not tell everyone that you are *too blessed to be stressed* when below the surface you are fuming at life. Whenever you are experiencing anger or bitterness, the overindulgence in food, shopping, or any other self-pacifying behaviors, will not fix the issue/issues that are bothering you. Stress-eating and stress-shopping are temporary bandages for a bigger issue. *"Cast thy burden upon the Lord, and he shall sustain thee: he shall never suffer the righteous to be moved"* (Psalms 55:22, KJV). Placing your feelings under the rug, over time will give birth to hatred and you will explode. Regardless of how you feel, go to your Heavenly Father. Be honest with Him. He already knows how you feel, and He also knows about the issue that is plaguing you. He is waiting for you to come. Going to your Heavenly Father conveys your need for His help and that you are dependent on Him. Give up your 'rights' to pretend that you are doing okay. Your Heavenly Father is not annoyed by your emotional-dump in His ears. The longer you spend harboring these feelings in your heart, the greater the power you will give the evil one to unravel your faith. Use your faith to squeeze the pent up emotion out of your spirit. *"Above all, taking the shield of faith, wherewith ye shall be able to quench all the fiery darts of the wicked"* (Ephesians 6: 16, KJV). Go to your Heavenly Father and tell Him where it hurts. If you cannot speak, then cry!!!!!!! He is undisturbed by YOU. In His eyes you are His only child, so you get all the 'daddy-time'. Go to Him.

ACCEPT MY WORSHIP

I cannot believe that I was chosen for such an honorable thing
Or that I was hand-selected by The King of Kings

I was just a seed in my mother's womb, and every fiber was woven to play a part in this holy scene
So, I must be careful in all I do and say, because my deeds are being recorded and by Him will be seen

This plan is orchestrated by a God so divine, who has all the power to destroy and that we cannot deny
Yet, He has restrained and humbled himself—what honor it is to please Him and so I willing comply

I am deeply touched that even though I am broken and bruised
That I was chosen by The King of Kings to be used
My body was intercepted to transport a living soul
O Lord may I be worthy and my name written in that scroll

I was created for this purpose, and my body was made a house of worship
To carry His glory and to accept His sovereignty and lordship
O Father, I humbly pray that my flaws do not deform my offspring
Because I was created for this purpose and my body is a living offering

WEEK 36

I am about the size of a head of romaine lettuce.

18.66in/47.4cm long

For he hath strengthened the bars of thy gates; he hath blessed thy children within thee.

Psalm 147: 13

Dear Mom,

I am in awe! An entire life is formed and housed in another life. Are you ready, Mom, to give me the name that you have been preparing? No pressure, our master designer, our Heavenly Father knows my name. He has been the originator and master designer of this beautiful journey. This week, I am approximately 6 pounds and measure 20 inches long. I have some not great news for you. My little butt is being filled with meconium- the sticky black substance which forms my first poop. Yuck! I know that it sounds yucky, but it means I am alive and doing very well. By the way, this week I am getting into my birthing position for my debut into your world. I am excited but it also means that this week I cannot do any somersaults. My movements are slowing down and I am counting down the days to see your world. Are you excited to meet me? I am totally thrilled to see and smell you. Laugh out loud (lol).

Dear Child,

Isaiah 40: 26, KJV declares, *"Lift up your eyes on high, and behold who hath created these things, that bringeth out their host by number: he calleth them all by names by the greatness of his might, for that he is strong in power; not one faileth"*. Child my child, The Divine One knows each star by its name. The Pistol Star is one of the brightest stars in the Milky Way and its luminosity is 3.3 million times that of the Sun. Its stellar wind is over 10 billion times stronger than the sun. Scientists report that they are uncertain of the age, mass, and future of this Pistol star. This star, my child, our God -your God knows by name. There is no star that is forgotten or unaccounted for as a result of God's failure. This prediction of uncertainty lies not on the part of the God who names each star by name. Since our God knows the names of approximately 200 billion trillion stars that are in the observable universe, why would not He know you, my child? He is even concerned with the smallest known star EBLM J0555-57Ab. It is recorded that this star was discovered in 2017 by the Wide Angle Search for Planets (WASP). Oh, my dear child, nothing is too big or too small for our God. The smallest star is known by Him and before EBLM J0555-57Ab was discovered in 2017, believe me, our God knew its whereabouts. You, my child is in His hands!

Dear Children,

Your Heavenly Father sees the big picture. The journey may not have been smooth or peachy all the days, but you should be confident in knowing that your Heavenly Father sees all the pieces of the puzzle. The master designer sees the finished product of your life. *"And we know that all things work together for good to them that love God, to them who are the called according to his purpose"* (Romans 8: 28, KJV). Even though things may seem as if the wheel is falling off the cart, and things are going awry and away from the planned course —*Trust your Heavenly Father.* His character has been proven to be trustworthy. He is not startled by chaos and unexplainable circumstances. Your Heavenly Father is in the midst of your calamity. *"Then Nebuchadnezzar the king was astonished, and rose up in haste, and spake, and said unto his counsellors, Did not we cast three men bound into the midst of the fire? They answered and said unto the king, True, O king. He answered and said, Lo, I see four men loose, walking in the midst of the fire, and they have no hurt; and the form of the fourth is like the Son of God"* (Daniel 3: 24-25, KJV). You may be unnerved by your circumstances, but your Heavenly Father is not. He is the fourth man in the fire with you. He ordained the fire, but He certainly did not start the fire. Nevertheless, He is in the fire with you, and He is commanding the fire not to burn you. The crisis of your life is going to fit in the *"all things work together for good to them that love God, to them who are the called according to His purpose."* The circumstances of your life will work TOGETHER for GOOD. The seemingly missing pieces of your puzzle are in the hands of your Heavenly Father. Your tests in your life are the bedrock of your testimony. Do not be mistaken by your Heavenly Father's silence and go off thinking that He is absent. His silence does NOT equate absence. He is in your '**ALL things work together**'. Do not run from your fires, your Heavenly Father is the fourth man, and He is in there with you. Rest in Him. You may leave this life-experience with the smell of smoke from your fire, but rest assured you will not be burnt.

WEEK 37

I am about the size of a winter melon.

19.13in/48.6cm long

For my thoughts are not your thoughts, neither are your ways my ways, saith the Lord. For as the heavens are higher than the earth, so are my ways higher than your ways, and my thoughts than your thoughts.

Isaiah 55: 8-9

Dear Mom,

This week, there is not much left to do other than put on some extra pounds. By design all the critical pieces of the puzzle are complete. At this stage Mom, all your food intake is going to be used for additional storage of fat. My *large* house has become my *tiny* house. I am totally out of space to move around. I am so sorry but this week I may have to jab you in your ribs or in your pelvis. I am truly not trying to hurt you. It is just my '*I am squished*' language and I am asking you to get up and move around. Since it is the 37th week, I will be reabsorbing some of my soft body hair and the white greasy skin coating. No worries, it is going into my little gut, and I will deposit into my first poop. What a treat! Sorry Mom......it is part of the mom duty list. I promise that I will make it up to you with lots of baby smooches.

Dear Child,

Creation speaks of a creator who is a master designer. The universe is a masterpiece. *"Who hath directed the Spirit of the Lord, or being his counselor hath taught him? With whom took he counsel, and who instructed him…..."* (Isaiah 40: 13 & 14b, KJV). All the details of the masterpiece are original. There is no plagiarism in His creation. You, my child, is an original. If you should ever get lost, the same God who is all powerful cannot replace you. There is only **ONE** of you. Doctors have finally gotten on the same page as the master designer and agreed that no two individuals who are alike— *heaven already knew this truth.* Our fingerprint is one of the uniqueness of humans. The sovereignty of our creator still dismissed the idea that identical twins would share the same traits. *In His wisdom, He polished the ridges and the lines of each fingerprint so that our fingerprints are completely different.* Even more fascinating is that our fingerprints remain the same from our birth until death. What a God! And He did not consult any doctors, scientists or any human form……..**His work is ORIGINAL**. By God's majestic power you my child exists. *Our Heavenly Father does not own a photocopy machine.* Laugh out loud! Each cell, nerve, tissue, organ, and body system echoes His masterful works. My child, I stand in amazement of the intricacies of your existence. In the first phase of your embryonic development, you were only ONE cell (a zygote) and as time elapsed the fertile egg rapidly divided into numerous cells all with a predetermined job description and a specialized function. My child, do I need to continue telling you how powerful our

Heavenly Father, the Master Designer truly is? The Godhead works in unity to ensure the specificity of each created being is accomplished. There are no medical malpractice claims to file……..there are no legal battles to fight over the ownership of His creative license. His created beings are patented. My child, you are stamped with His seal of divinity. You are His!

Dear Children,

A disconnected power cord from its source of power is futile. A brand-new car that is parked in a garage but has no fuel is pointless. Your life will feel and become hopeless when you are disconnected from your Heavenly Father. Your life will feel and become empty when you are void of your Heavenly Father's presence. Your Heavenly Father has not left His space of existence—*you left*. You drifted and because you drifted from His presence, you are feeling and becoming disappointed with your life. In His presence there is restoration. You may have suffered losses in your life and so you thought that disconnecting from the source of power would allow you to work out some things for yourself. The truth is, your decision is not aligned to the character of your Heavenly Father. He is a restorer!

Restoration of blessings: *"For your shame ye shall have double"* (Isaiah 61:7a, KJV).

Restoration of wholeness: *"But the God of all grace, who hath called us unto his eternal glory by Christ Jesus, after that ye have suffered a while, make you perfect, stablish, strengthen, settle you"* (1 Peter 5: 10, KJV).

Restoration of health: *"For I will restore health unto thee, and I will heal thee of thy wounds, saith the Lord;...."* (Jeremiah 30:17a, KJV).

Restoration of relationship: *"If my people, which are called by my name, shall humble themselves, and pray, and seek my face, and turn from their wicked ways; then will I hear from heaven, and will forgive their sin, and will heal their land"* (2 Chronicles 7:14, KJV).

Your idea of drifting will remove you from the nourishment of your Heavenly Father's presence. Restoration of your hope, your faith, your joy and your confidence can only be found in your Heavenly Father's presence. Do not waste your time creating your own life away from Him. The longer you stay away from Him the more difficult it is for you to accept your Heavenly Father's restoration. Dismiss your desire to stay away from Him. He awaits you!

WEEK 38

I am about the size of a rhubarb.

19.61in/49.8cm long

Listen, O isles, unto me; and hearken, ye people, from far; The Lord hath called me from the womb; from the bowels of my mother hath he made mention of my name.

Isaiah 49:1

Dear Mom,

This week you may be feeling worried that I will never come fast enough. Relax…...I am coming home to you. Try not to be overwhelmed. Reactivate your faith and be confident that the master planner is going to bring me home safely. Remember, we are a part of a divine plan. We are in His hands. Each passing day, I am laying down fat under my skin. Most of my days, I am just sleeping and hanging out in my space that once felt like a king-size bed (now it feels like a twin-size bed). I am slowing down, and it feels like you are also slowing down. You are getting bigger, and I am definitely getting bigger. What a trip! We are coming to the end of a wonderful journey. I feel so connected to you—*you are MY mom.*

Dear Child,

As we are near the ending weeks of this journey, I find myself wishing that I could go back in time and correct some of my ME-ways. The ways that were *me-centric.* My focus was centered around pleasing how I felt rather than how I grew as a result of His presence. I spent a great deal of time fixated on how I felt and looked, while secretly wishing that I felt and looked 'better'. Oftentimes, I felt anxious because I was bringing things from the future into the present. I spent days imprisoned by the '*what ifs*', and my child, they were weighing me down. I was disconnected from the true source of power. I had the mindset that you were **mine**. *I later became aware that you are HIS and you are simply a gift to me.* However, this day reminds me that our Heavenly Father does not need my approval to pour out His favor on your life. As mothers, we follow the customs of society that dictates that babies are to be dedicated to God upon their birth and in most cases approximately between 4 and 8 months old. On the 38th week of this journey, I am shouting from the mountain top, *"dedication must be done while the child is still in the womb!"* Why should mothers and fathers withhold their child from The Giver of the blessing? *"For this child I prayed; and the Lord hath given me my petition which I asked of him: Therefore also I have lent him to the Lord; as long as he liveth he shall be lent to the Lord"* (1 Samuel 1: 27 & 28, KJV). Relinquishing my grip on you is becoming more difficult, my child. The nearer we get to the end of this journey, the more I want to fasten my grip on you. How did Hannah return her child to The Lord? What was her mindset? She weaned and then returned that which God had given her. My dear little one, I am struggling with that kind of faith—*the kind of faith that fully submits*. Indeed, you are a gift that belongs to The Lord, and I now realize that the commitment of returning you to Him must be done before you enter my world. My dear little one, as I approach the second to last week of a normal pregnancy journey, I am choosing to submit my **ME**-ness. This tendency of stamping everything with my *me-agenda* stifles my faith to trust that you are in His care. My desire to hover over you like a helicopter is edging on the side of idolatry. God must always be above my interjections. Sweet little one, I am placing you fully in His hands. *"It is he that hath made us, and not we ourselves; we are HIS people"* (Psalm 100: 3b, KJV).

Dear Children,

Taking on the challenges of this world on your own is the recipe for self-destruction. Bringing your fears of the future into your today is turmoil. Some of the pain you are facing is preloaded from your anxious mind wondering about your tomorrow. Your 'humanness' is riddled with fear, and your fear of the future is disrupting your today. This habit of living in the future is resulting in an unthankful heart. You are unable to be thankful because your worries are focused on the negatives. It is impossible to be thankful when you are facing the *hypothesized problems* of the future. A heart of gratitude cannot be realized when you wander into fear. *"Let not your heart be troubled, neither let it be afraid"* (John 14: 27b, KJV). As soon as your mind unwraps a hypothesized problem, erase it by praising your Heavenly Father. A hypothesized problem is a problem that has been conjured up in your mind, but it has not even occurred. It is a *what-if* mental battle. For example: if I do not have enough money to pay my bills then I will be homeless. This type of mental battle deletes God from the picture. It hurls you into the unknown and supplies you with a vast number of proposed scenarios none of which has happened. This battle of the mind is seated in the camp of the evil one satan. He—*satan*, was declared by your Heavenly Father as the *father of lies*. His most valuable tool that he uses to throw you off your axis is anxiety and unfounded worry. In moments when you are caught in the middle of a mental battle, turn to your Heavenly Father and begin expressing your thankfulness for your 'todays'. *"For God hath not given us the spirit of fear; but of power, and of love, and of a sound mind"* (2 Timothy 1:7, KJV). Resist the habit of compounding your life with unnecessary pain. Start a habit of thanking your Heavenly Father for your life. Whether or not (by your standards) your life is on course, find at least one thing that could have been worse. Even if you cannot find anything to be thankful for, try to find one thing that you can express gratitude for not having or being in a particular situation.

BE IT UNTO ME

A sacred journey and so it began

I questioned myself but lo it was already done

A life within me—God's borrowed breath

I knew that He loved me, but I never understood the depth

O my child, may you be perfect, was my silent plea

But my heart overrode my selfishness, and I cried, "Lord, according to thy word, be it unto me"

Your tiny hands and feet were so perfectly designed

And then in that moment I understood that this plan was beautiful and divine

I never said another idle word, nor did I fret

Because heaven was beside me, so the powers of darkness was no longer a threat

I curtailed my worries and banished my fears

I knew that even though it was silent, my Heavenly Father still hears

For every heartbeat I felt, I knew you were not mine

A borrowed breath was only for a season and a gift for a time

My body was sacrificed on an altar of love

Lord, according to thy word, be it unto me and that was enough

WEEK 39

I am about the size of a small pumpkin.

19.96in/50.7cm long

Fear thou not; for I am with thee: be not dismayed; for I am thy God: I will strengthen thee; yea, I will help thee; yea, I will uphold thee with the right hand of my righteousness.

Isaiah 41:10

Dear Mom,

Week 39 is a big week in Baby Land. If I am your first baby, it is highly likely that I may enter your world later than you had anticipated. Be open-minded and have faith and trust that we are both in the hands of The Divine One who started this journey. He has never failed us because He **cannot** fail. Having witnessed the intricacies throughout this journey we should be confident that we are in good hands. As you await my arrival, start playing music and sing to me. I can hear your sweet voice. Read to me; I am fond of stories. This early stimulation increases the likelihood that I will be a clever human being. By the way, if you have not done so already, dedicate my life to The Lord. *I am here because of Him*!

Dear Child,

This week, I have a deeper realization that our Heavenly Father loves us. He is delighted to be our father. I know that we are still doing well on this journey because of His watchful eye on our lives. *"I will lift up mine eyes unto the hills, from whence cometh my help. My help cometh from the Lord, which made heaven and earth. He will not suffer thy foot to be moved: he that keepeth thee will not slumber. Behold, he that keepeth Israel shall neither slumber nor sleep. The Lord is thy keeper......"* (Psalm 121: 1-5a, KJV). Throughout these weeks, we have been more than cared for. Oh, my child, He is far better to you than I can ever be. He who keeps the universe, does not slumber nor sleep. Our God does not take a nap. He does not own a pair of pajamas. My sweet little one, He is not inattentive to our needs. He is fully aware of our wellbeing. I cannot even imagine trusting another person. All my life, He has been faithful to me, and I am confident that He will be faithful to you. I am troubled by the thought that humanity has bought into the enemy's lie that our God cannot be trusted. It is the plan of the devil to get us to doubt the character of our Heavenly Father. The devil did the same game in heaven, which ultimately caused a riot in heaven. What gave the devil ulcers was God's response of sending his ONLY child to die for our sins and to show us how to live a sinless life. The gift of God's son dying for us is wonderful but even more wonderful is showing us that to navigate life requires COMPLETE dependence on His father. My dear child, as we transition to another phase, I am handing over the reins to our Father and adopting Jesus' model of living. My desire for you, my child, is that you will live a victorious life. This victory over sin and defeat is found in the complete allegiance to the script that Jesus himself used—*not my will but my Father's will be done.* My dear little one, I pray that as your development was fully within the care of The Holy One of Israel, that when you enter my world that you will allow Him full access to your life and that you will include him in every facet of your life. The day is fastly approaching but remember we are submitting our will and accepting His purpose for our lives.

Dear Children,

Do not follow your old mode of operations and exclude your Heavenly Father from your plans. Do not get into the habit of including Him in the big things while shunning Him from the minuscule details of your life. It is the 'little things' that your Heavenly Father is excluded from, that usually destroy lives. He wants to be God over **all** areas of your life. Why are you excluding Him from areas of your life? *"Whither shall I go from thy spirit? or whither shall I flee from thy presence? If I ascend up into heaven, thou art there: if I make my bed in hell, behold, thou art there. If I take the wings of the morning, and dwell in the uttermost parts of the sea; Even there shall thy hand lead me, and thy right hand shall hold me"* (Psalms 139: 7-10, KJV). **Exclusion leads to isolation** which in turn causes you to tackle life's challenges alone. Release every area of your life to your Heavenly Father. Prayer is a sacred time for you to invite Him into your space. *Prayer gives heaven permission to act on your behalf.* This medium of communication between heaven and earth is an opportunity for the angels to receive orders to fight your battles. Only one-third of the angels were cast out of heaven with the evil one. Therefore, there are two-thirds of the host of angels that remained in heaven. That means there are more on your side than those against you. Angels are waiting to fight your battles. Do not impose your own obstacles and barricade yourself from receiving divine help. *"He shall call upon me, and I will answer him: I will be with him in trouble; I will deliver him, and honour him"* (Psalm 91: 15, KJV). Heaven awaits your cry for help. **You are not interrupting heaven's schedule.**

WEEK 40

I am about the size of a growing pumpkin.

20.16in/51.2cm long

Take heed that ye despise not one of these little ones; for I say unto you, That in heaven their angels do always behold the face of my Father which is in heaven.

Matthew 18:10

Dear Mom,

Mom oh Mom! The official end of our journey is finally here. You may start feeling lots of Braxton Hicks contractions. If they are too bothersome, try taking a warm shower and b-r-e-a-t-h…...I am not trying to hurt you. My arrival is sure, and I am making little knocks on your door. You may feel tired of waiting but I am not bothered by the wait. I have been a part of a divine orchestration and waiting no longer bothers me. Rest in His promise. Everything is under His control and the 40th week is a part of His plan. Why worry, be happy! This week is a part of the journey, and you and I are a part of His will.

Dear Child,

Oh, my sweetheart, my little one, the end of the journey is upon us. I am somewhat anxious about your birth. Will it be a smooth one? Little one, should I worry, or should I rest in our Heavenly Father? What was the quote attributed to Erma Bombeck? *"Worry is like a rocking chair; it gives you something to do but it doesn't get you anywhere."* One side of me wants to worry but the other side yells, "We are in God's hands!" I am reminded that the Lord is my shepherd. I will not lack anything. I am reminded of Psalm 23. *"Yea, though I walk through the valley of the shadow of death, I will fear no evil: for thou art with me; thy rod and thy staff they comfort me"* (Psalm 23: 4, KJV). So, I am choosing to rest in our Heavenly Father because throughout the divine script I can find no fault with Him. There is not one recorded time that He has never failed or forgotten His children. History has proven over and over that He never fails. So, this week, I have decided to place my full confidence in Him. He saw you before you were even formed. He saw you before I met your father. He saw you before my mother and father met. He saw you before my grandfather and grandmother met. He saw you before my ancestors existed. He **SAW** you and cared for you. So, I relinquish my fears and my doubts, and I will place my trust in him. Oh, my little one, oh my little one you were just a tiny cell, and now you are fully ready to be delivered. Who could it be but the Most High God, who took care of you before you were even formed. *"Who is this King of glory? The Lord strong and mighty, the Lord mighty in battle. He is the King of Glory"* (Psalm 24: 8, KJV). I cannot take credit for anything that I have done on this journey. I can only declare that only He is to be worshiped and served. My dear child, only our Heavenly Father is to be worshiped!

Dear Children,

This journey is coming to an end and the lessons that were embedded in the experience were intended to be beneficial to your spiritual and personal growth. Despite the rapid changes that you went through, your Heavenly Father remained constant. You may still be feeling inadequate to handle the responsibilities that are ahead, but your Heavenly Father is with you. The weaker you are, the more He will step in and show His strength. God is interested in people who do not feel equipped. He specializes in equipping those He calls. If your academic, financial, social or political achievements are sufficient, then you have no need for your Heavenly Father. He is not going to violate your decision to leave Him out of your life when you feel adequate to do life outside of Him. He will remain in the background and allow you to 'live' your life. Your addiction to fix everything without your Heavenly Father's input and to operate your life in a *no-need-for-God* manner, is troubling. A life lived outside of God is the recipe for unprecedented turmoil. Challenges are layered in everyone's lives but to a believer in Jesus Christ, challenges are building blocks for character. When you have a deep understanding of the relentless effort that heaven invests in chasing after you, you will begin gaining an awareness that it pays to serve Jesus. Reflect on this journey and think about how many times your Heavenly Father has proven how much He loves you. He is concerned that you are not letting Him love you and guide you throughout your life. The distance between you and your Heavenly Father is causing a gap in the relationship. The end result is heartache and sorrow. Notwithstanding, He is waiting for you to run back into His arms. Your human cynicism as to why your Heavenly Father wants to be a part of your life, is hindering you from seeing the pureness in His love. "*The Lord hath appeared of old unto me, saying, Yea, I have loved thee with an everlasting love: therefore with lovingkindness have I drawn thee*" (Jeremiah 31: 3, KJV). Even though you have relegated your Heavenly Father to the background of your life, He and heaven are cheering you on. "*..............lo, I am with you always, even unto the end of the world. Amen*" (Matthew 28: 20, KJV).

WEEK 41

I am about the size of a watermelon.

20.35in/51.5cm long

Hearken unto me, O house of Jacob, and all the remnant of the house of Israel, which are borne by me from the belly, which are carried from the womb:

Isaiah 46:3

Dear Mom,

Frustration is not welcomed on this journey. Faith requires patience and trust. You cannot experience this faith unless you tap into your *patience-bank.* I know the suggested 40th (fortieth week) week has passed, and everyone is asking where I am. Tell them, my arrival is not in our control; *everything is a part of a divine plan.* One thing is for sure, there will be a delivery date and that date has been decided on by The Almighty One. Most of my lanugo and the white greasy substance on my skin has been reabsorbed and stored into my little gut. No worries…….my first poop will clean out all the waste out of my body. Be prepared for a very stinky deposit. At this stage of the journey, I know you will not be bothered by those details. I am fully developed, and I am ready to breathe and cry my first tear. I know it is challenging to relax, but try to focus on who is in control. Our Heavenly Father *has us in the palm of His hands.*

Dear Child,

This must be the week!!!!! According to the medical scripts, the final leg of the journey has already passed. Of course, you and I now know that the master designer will not consult my doctors regarding your birth. Oh, my baby, your birth is not delayed, it is occurring in accordance with the plans of the master designer. If I have trusted our Heavenly Father for the past forty weeks, should I start distrusting him NOW? Oh, my child, *"Being confident of this very thing, that he which hath begun a good work in you will perform it……….."* (Philippians 1:6, KJV). I am secured in my faith in The Lord. In the grand divine plan, you are not overdue. This journey has gifted me the beauty of staying in our Heavenly Father's presence. As the days progress and the calendar passes the 40th (fortieth) week, I am turning my face in God's presence. His presence is a frozen moment in time when my anxiety ceases, my fears are paralyzed, and my worries are disabled. In His presence, I am given a blank check that declares that ALL IS WELL. Oh, my little one, be of good cheer. The Holy One of Israel has promised us that he will NEVER leave us or forsake us. *"God is not a man, that he should lie; neither the son of man, that he should repent: hath he said, and shall he not do it? or hath he spoken, and shall he not make it good?"* (Numbers 23: 19, KJV). My child, we are not alone on this journey. The God of Jacob is our Refuge and our Strength. Oh, fear not, do not worry your little head……. your mom has placed you in the hands of a God

173

that cannot fail. Remember that our journey was encrypted with faith, so let us not lose confidence in the master designer's promises. In just a little while you will enter my world. You are fully in His hands! *"..........and ye know in all your hearts and in all your souls, that not one thing hath failed of all the good things which the Lord your God spake concerning you; all are come to pass unto you, and not one thing hath failed thereof"* (Joshua 23:14b, KJV). Have no fear, Jehovah God is here!

Dear Children,

He loves you regardless of your failures. You do not have to buy your Heavenly Father's love. This father has made a covenant with His children that He will keep until eternity. His covenant is an eternal contract. There is nothing that you can do or do not do to undo His decision. Your accomplishments, your achievements, and your decisions cannot interfere with the underwriter's (which is your Heavenly Father) covenant. *"Know therefore that the Lord thy God, he is God, the faithful God, which keepeth covenant and mercy with them that love him and keep his commandments to a thousand generations;"* (Deuteronomy 7: 9, KJV). The terms of the contract (covenant) were not written by any earthly being. Having knowledge of the evil which plagues humanity, only a God of love would make this contractual decision to bind His heart to ours for eternity. What a loving Father! This journey is a stage on which your Heaven Father acted out the merits of His covenant that He has with you. He has demonstrated to you countless times that His plans and thoughts towards you are good. In His words you will find that His covenant is layered with promises. *"But the mercy of the Lord is from everlasting to everlasting upon them that fear him, and his righteousness unto children's children;..."* (Psalms 103:17a, KJV). Stay in His presence to gain an understanding of His role in this covenant which He made with humanity. A steady diet of His presence will reveal His sovereignty down through ages. You will realize that in the historical pages, each generation testified of this same covenant keeping God. Your Heavenly Father has watched His people wander off from Him to worship idols made out of stone and wood, and still His covenant remained steadfast. You may have some troubling thoughts about your future, but you can rest assured that He will not reject you. *"Be strong and of a good courage, fear not, nor be afraid of them: for the Lord thy God, he it is that doth go with thee; he will not fail thee, nor forsake thee"* (Deuteronomy

31: 6, KJV). There is a calmness in knowing that your Heavenly Father's covenant is non-negotiable, does not expire, or needs to be justified by you having a good credit score. Be still and let your mind rest upon this truth. Let the fragrance of this truth saturate your worrisome mind. Your failure to fully comprehend the weight of your Heavenly Father's covenant with you is having adverse effects on how you move through life. You often magnify your problems instead of magnifying your God. You tend to forget your worth and how much your Heavenly Father values you. These self-destructive behaviors are depleting your *faith-funds*, and you are often left overdrawn and operating in the negative. Allow this covenant keeper to deposit in you His peace so you can calm your mind. *"For the mountains shall depart, and the hills be removed; but my kindness shall not depart from thee, neither shall the covenant of my peace be removed, saith the Lord that hath mercy on thee"* (Isaiah 54: 10, KJV).

A POSTURE OF PRAISE

You are The Potter, and I am the clay
My body is yours Lord so use it as you may
I empty myself of selfishness and pride
O may I be found worthy and in me abide

Why I was chosen is not for me to know
O that my life would please you and to others my love show
This journey has been planned, and the details are in place
There is nothing that is amiss or wandering in space

This child is mine to carry for the fullness of days
And may my imperfections be blotted out and my mouth filled with praise

My body was molded for a heavenly transaction as this
And nothing is too hard for you Lord is what my soul admits

WEEK 42

I am about the size of a jackfruit.

20.28in/51.3cm long

And even to your old age I am he; and even to hoar hairs will I carry you: I have made, and I will bear; even I will carry, and will deliver you.

Isaiah 46:4

Dear Mom,

I know that there is nothing humorous about being overdue. You can choose to be frustrated and raise your stress level. Or you can trust that my arrival is yet another detail in the divine plan. Either way, you or I do not control our lives. My skin may be a little dry because the white greasy substance has been absorbed; but it is nothing that a little olive oil cannot fix. I will admit that I am going to be hungry when I enter your world because I have not been fed as well by my placenta. Not to worry though…...The master designer has been caring and sustaining me. He has already thought about every little detail. This is not a surprise to Him. **Faith is knowing that He is in control and leaving every detail to Him**. Faith is letting God work out His master plan and trusting His purpose. I may be delayed but I am still here. I am arriving at the time that was recorded in the plan. Remember, my master designer is not constrained by time.

Dear Child,

It is the 42nd (forty-second week) and I am choosing to embed in my spirit the words that are True and Faithful. I will not allow fear to interrupt my time in His presence. I will infuse my spirit with the living word of God. Each day I will declare:

"Delight thyself also in the Lord: and he shall give thee the desires of thine heart. Commit thy way unto the Lord; TRUST ALSO IN HIM; and he shall bring it to pass" (Psalm 37: 4 & 5, KJV).

"Every word of God is pure: he is a shield unto them that PUT THEIR TRUST IN HIM" (Proverbs 30:5-6, KJV).

"FEAR THOU NOT; for I am with thee:" (Isaiah 41:10a, KJV).

"REST IN THE LORD, and wait patiently for him:" (Psalm 37: 7a, KJV).

Little one, I will TRUST —*which ignites my faith to do something rather than dragging myself throughout this week*. I will resist the urge to let my mind wander. Instead I will use my energy to fuel my spirit NOT to fear. The buzz around here is subtly seeking to trigger an anxious spirit. But fear speaks against the character of our God. Fear jeopardizes my spiritual health. This week I will default to trust. I am officially placing a **D**o **N**ot **R**esuscitate (DNR) message over my *fear-gene*. I have no desire to place my fear on a *life-supporting* machine. I want fear to be deleted from my life.

Oh, my child, I cannot wait to see your beautiful face. I am still amazed that I was chosen to carry you. I was chosen by heaven to be your mom. Oh, little one.........I will REST and wait patiently for your entrance. The Divine One, the Master Designer has ordained this week as the completion of a masterpiece. I love you so much......I cannot wait to hold you, my love. By the way, our Heavenly father is just as involved in my world as He is your world. He is omnipresent— *present everywhere at the same time.* He is omniscient—*knows our past, present, and future.* He is omnipotent—*has unlimited power and can do anything.* What a mighty God!

Dear Children,

The timing of God is **The TIME**! Your Heavenly Father is not bound by time so He is never late. God does not operate in the *chronos* time (minutes, days, months, years, etc.) as humans do. God resides in the *kairos* time span. Kairos, an ancient Greek word which signifies the opportune, right and critical time. It is a time that things just show up—*never late, never too early; it is just the RIGHT time.* Kairos time piece studies the nuances of a situation while diminishing the chronos operations. A kairos dealer is not distracted by the demands of the chronos operations because it is a RIGHT time dealer. Understanding the kairos elements will relieve your worries about your Heavenly perceived late arrival in your situations. When you chain yourself to the chronos time clock, you will become frustrated and speak evil of your Heavenly Father. Chronos time will also lead to covetousness because you want your life to match up to your circle of influence. Unthankfulness, bitterness, and self-loathing behaviors are just a few of the evils that can spill over from entering a contract with chronos timepiece. Chronos time downplays the role of your Heavenly Father in your life. You are so fixated on the *When* that you will begin to stress yourself with the **Whys**. Why now? You are plagued with questions such as "Why is there a delay?" Listen........your Heavenly Father is asking you, "But whose standard are you measuring what and when something should happen in your life?"

"For the vision is yet for an appointed time, but at the end it shall speak, and not lie: though it tarry, wait for it; because it will surely come, it will not tarry" (Habakkuk 2: 3, KJV).

"Rest in the Lord, and wait patiently for him: fret not thyself because of him who prospereth in his way......." (Psalms 37: 7a, KJV).

"For my thoughts are not your thoughts, neither are your ways my ways, saith the Lord. For as the heavens are higher than the earth, so are my ways higher than your ways, and my thoughts than your thoughts" (Isaiah 55: 8-9, KJV).

It is all GOD'S TIMING……..***your Heavenly Father knows what is best***. Rest in Him!

ABOUT THE BOOK

To carry a child into this world is such a sacred experience—an experience that encourages expectant mothers to take note of and revere a divine transaction between heaven and earth. Pregnancy symbolizes an incubated space where divinity partners with earthly beings and gives expectant mothers the opportunity to encode their imprints on a living soul. In this book, *God, Mommy and Me: Our Unscripted Conversations*, the author Dr. KB gives voice to the unborn world which signals to our shifting culture that the sovereignty of God is cradled in every unborn's DNA. As the unborn speaks, the volume and sensitivity of the expectant mother's awareness peaks and she begins to sense that the life that she is carrying is more than just a physical being—**it is a living soul.** Through this awareness, she opens up her heart to hear her Heavenly Father's soft tones of guidance and at times pruning, as He brings to light unpolished details of her character that has the power to deform the unborn's soul. As Mom unmutes her Heavenly Father's voice, she recognizes that He has always been with her, and it is then she enters her role of being just His daughter—His child. *As this journey unfolds, she begins to redefine her Heavenly Father's instructions as acts of love and no longer sees His instruction as acts of control. Now, she is fascinated by the virtue of submission and welcomes His plans for both her life and her unborn child's existence.*

With every stroke of the author's brush, *God, Mommy and Me: Our Unscripted Conversations* emerges as a declarative portrait that seamlessly reveals the link between the sacredness of an unborn's life and the beautiful gift of eternal life.

www.ingramcontent.com/pod-product-compliance
Lightning Source LLC
Chambersburg PA
CBHW061748120626
46550CB00005B/1933